Mikoyan's Piston-Engined Fighters

Yefim Gordon and Keith Dexter

MIDLAND
An imprint of
Ian Allan Publishing

Mikoyan's Piston-Engined Fighters
© 2003 Yefim Gordon
ISBN 1 85780 160 1

Published by Midland Publishing
4 Watling Drive, Hinckley, LE10 3EY, England
Tel: 01455 254 490   Fax: 01455 254 495
E-mail: midlandbooks@compuserve.com

Midland Publishing is an imprint of
Ian Allan Publishing Ltd

Worldwide distribution (except North America):
Midland Counties Publications
4 Watling Drive, Hinckley, LE10 3EY, England
Telephone: 01455 254 450   Fax: 01455 233 737
E-mail: midlandbooks@compuserve.com
www.midlandcountiessuperstore.com

North American trade distribution:
Specialty Press Publishers & Wholesalers Inc.
39966 Grand Avenue, North Branch, MN 55056, USA
Tel: 651 277 1400   Fax: 651 277 1203
Toll free telephone: 800 895 4585
www.specialtypress.com

© 2003 Midland Publishing
Design concept and layout by
Polygon Press Ltd. (Moscow, Russia)
Edited by Dmitriy Komissarov
Line drawings by Andrey Yurgenson
Colour artwork by Valentin Vetlitskiy

This book is illustrated with photos from
the archives of Yefim Gordon, RSK MiG and
the Russian Aviation Research Trust

Printed in England by Ian Allan Printing Ltd
Riverdene Business Park, Molesey Road,
Hersham, Surrey, KT12 4RG

All rights reserved. No part of this publication
may be reproduced, stored in a retrieval
system, transmitted in any form or by any
means, electronic, mechanical or photo-copied,
recorded or otherwise, without the written
permission of the publishers.

Contents

Introduction 3
1. Birth of a Famous Brand 5
2. MIkoyan Makes His Mark:
   The First Major Production Version . 19
3. The MiG-3 in Action 33
4. Experimental Versions 51
5. To Build a Better 'Three':
   The I-230 Series 63
6. A New Line Emerges:
   The I-220 Series 73
7. The 'Half-Jet': Mikoyan's First
   Step Towards Jet Propulsion 95
8. The First Mikoyan Twin 95

   Line drawings 112
   Colour drawings 122

Title page: A pair of strike-configured MiG-3s carrying RS-82 rockets. Note the open cockpit canopies and the extended tailwheels.

Below: The flight line of the 12th Guards Fighter Regiment, a unit equipped with the MiG-3, in March 1942. Curiously, some aircraft never got winter camouflage.

Introduction

In the second half of the twentieth century the name 'MiG' was used generically in the West to embrace any type of Soviet fighter aircraft. The eponym is derived from, and a tribute to, the aircraft design bureau of Artyom Ivanovich Mikoyan and Mikhail Iosifovich Gurevich; the 'i' being the Russian word for 'and'. Soviet and now Russian aircraft bear the name of the design bureau rather than that of the manufacturing plant. Created in 1939, the MiG design bureau was formed at a time when the Soviet leader Iosif V. Stalin, already irritated by the acknowledged superiority of the German Messerschmitt Bf 109 fighter over Soviet types in the late stages of the Spanish Civil War, became increasingly incensed that not enough was being done to redress the balance. His immediate response was to allocate more design bureaux to promising younger designers.

One person to benefit from the decision was Artyom Mikoyan, born in Sanaïn, a small village in Armenia in 1905, who trained as an engineer at the Krasnyy Aksai factory in Rostov-on-Don. After completing his national service in the army and working for a while as a mechanic in Moscow, he entered the Air Force Academy named after Nikolay Ye. Zhukovskyy where he was awarded his pilot's licence and also became an accomplished parachutist. In 1939 he was appointed the representative of the VVS (*Voyenno-voz-dooshnyye seely*) at *zavod* (factory) No.1 imeni Aviakhima (named in 1925 after the Osoaviakhim organisation which supported the Air Force and the chemical industry) at Khodynka airfield, then in a north-western suburb of Moscow (the place is now virtually right in the centre of the city). He was a VVS officer responsible for monitoring, on behalf of the Air Force, the quality of aircraft before they left the plant. He was also involved with the factory management in improving the efficiency of the production line of the Polikarpov I-153 biplane fighters then being manufactured at the plant.

Mikhail Gurevich was born in Khar'kov in the Ukraine where his studies of mathematics at the university terminated abruptly in 1913 with his expulsion as a revolutionary, in consequence of which he entered Montpellier University in France. Returning home after the October Revolution of 1917, he completed his mathematical studies and, in addition, aeronautical engineering at Khar'kov before working in succession at several aircraft design bureaux. After visiting the USA in 1937 with a team to negotiate a licence to produce the Douglas DC-3 airliner, he returned to Russia and helped launch production of the Soviet version. (It was designated PS-84 to indicate *passazheerskiy samolyot* (passenger aircraft) built by *zavod* No.84, which was then located in Khimki, a northern suburb of Moscow. Later, when the plant was evacuated to Tashkent, this aeroplane was redesignated Li-2 in honour of Boris F. Lisunov, the project's chief engineer.) Towards the end of 1938, Gurevich joined the Polikarpov design bureau based at *zavod* No.1 as head of the Projects Department, a move which introduced him to Mikoyan.

Mikhail Iosifovich Gurevich (left) and Artyom Ivanovich Mikoyan, the 'fathers' of the MiG brand, with a model of the MiG-3 in post-war years.

Now we have to turn our attention to another notable person. Nikolai N. Polikarpov became known as the 'King of Fighters' as a result of his success in designing not only the I-3, I-5, I-15, I-15*bis* and I-153 biplane fighters but also the I-16, the world's first cantilever monoplane fighter to enter service with an enclosed cockpit and retractable undercarriage. Unfortunately for him his proposed successor to the I-16, the I-180, was not successful, principally because of an underdeveloped engine and, after two disastrous crashes, he fell even further out of favour with Stalin. In early 1939 Polikarpov started work on a new monoplane fighter with an in-line liquid-cooled engine provisionally designated *Samolyot* 'Kh' (Aircraft 'Kh'; Kh, the 22nd letter of the Russian alphabet, was used as a codename.) In November 1939, returning

This is how the Moscow Machinery Plant No.155 (the seat of the MIkoyan/Gurevich design bureau) looked in the 1940s.

from a visit to Germany as part of a trade delegation, he was dismayed to find that a new OKO (***op**ytno-**konstrook**torskiy ot**del*** – Experimental Design Department) had been formed in *zavod* No 1. It was to be led by the young Artyom Mikoyan but Polikarpov was to remain chief designer of the factory. Furthermore, the OKO had been entrusted with the job of continuing the design of the *Samolyot* 'Kh' – later to become the I-200 and, after the start of serial production, the MiG-1.

In an attempt to pre-empt any imposed government decision, a commission had been set up in November by the factory management to decide which type of aircraft should replace the Polikarpov I-153 biplane then in production. At this time Polikarpov was still in Germany but, fortunately for him, his team was able to persuade the commission that *Samolyot* 'Kh' was a better proposition than its original choice, the Yakovlev I-26 (which later entered production as the Yak-1). To expedite the design work the factory management also set up their own design department with the clear intention of removing control of this work from Polikarpov who was presented with a *fait accompli* on his return from Germany. As Chief Designer of *zavod* No.1 and head of his own OKB (***op**ytno-**konstrook**torskoye **byuro*** – design bureau) he was, to say the least, displeased when he returned to find a cuckoo in his nest.

Polikarpov acknowledged that his past successes had made him many enemies and, after initial resistance, accepted the situation; no doubt consoling himself with the fact that, in any case, he had a fighter prototype, the radial-engined I-185, almost ready for its first flight.

His resistance to change was understandable as about 80 of his staff had been transferred to the new OKO, including M. I. Gurevich and V. A. Romodin, both senior designers working on *Samolyot* 'Kh' and both now assistants to Mikoyan. Another blow to Polikarpov's pride came when Mikoyan was also made Deputy Chief Designer of *zavod* No.1 on 14th December 1939 with a direct line of responsibility to the factory director, rather than to him. The OKO was officially promulgated by the NKAP (*Narodnyy komissariat aviatsionnoy promyshlennosti* – People's Commissariat (ie, Ministry) of the Aircraft Industry) on 8th December 1939. Obliged to continue with a diminished team, Polikarpov was transferred in July 1940 to a new but much smaller **Op**ytnyy ***za**vod* No.51 (experimental factory) at Khodynka, adjacent to *zavod* No.1.

There have been suggestions that Artyom Mikoyan was favoured because his elder brother Anastas was deputy chairman of Sovnarkom (Council of People's Commissars) and People's Commissar for External Trade. Although this relationship was advantageous, the original suggestion to promote him was not prompted by Stalin but by P. A. Voronin, Director of *zavod* No.1, and Pyotr V. Dement'yev, his deputy and chief engineer, both of whom had been impressed by his work at the factory. These two men had been instrumental in displacing Polikarpov from *zavod* No.1 and wanted to make sure that he did not complete the design of the next aircraft that was most likely to be mass-produced there. This may not have been personal animosity but rather concern that Polikarpov was attempting to design too many different types at the same time to the detriment of their factory.

Artyom Mikoyan, only 34 years of age at the time, understandably grasped this opportunity of promotion but, recognising his own lack of design experience, insisted on Gurevich as his principal deputy and was willing to share the credit with him.

Another part of the Mikoyan OKB's premises.

Chapter 1
Birth of a Famous Brand

I-200 (MiG-1, *Samolyot* 'Kh' and *izdeliye* 61)

The staff of the newly formed OKO *zavoda* No.1 (OKO of factory No.1) or OKO-1 were able from 25th November 1939 to concentrate their efforts on the new task: the creation of an interceptor with optimum performance at 6,000 m (19,700 ft). Controversy has arisen concerning the exact amount of work undertaken by Polikarpov's team before the design was appropriated by OKO-1. Understandably the event created a great deal of resentment and, even to this day, supporters of both sides stake a claim for the lion's share of the work. Certainly, Polikarpov was responsible for the initial specification and preliminary sketches for which he was later awarded the State Prize, but the remainder of the design work was completed under Mikoyan. Instead of debating which of these two leaders should be awarded the glory it seems more sensible to remember that Gurevich and Romodin, to name but two, were involved from the start of the project to its completion. *Samolyot* 'Kh', as it was originally known within the Polikarpov OKB, was renamed I-200; in line with VVS practice of designating their aircraft according to function, 'I' represented *istrebitel'*, fighter. Within *zavod* No.1 the type was known as *izdeliye* (article) 61 and therefore marked as such on most engineering drawings.

To achieve the required performance the Mikulin AM-37, a new engine still undergoing tests, had been selected for its promise of 1,400 hp (1,030 kW) at 6,000 m (19,700 ft). Preliminary calculations from a report by V. A. Romodin dated 8th December 1939 and addressed to the NKAP, GK NII VVS (*Gosoodarstvenny krasnoznamyonnyy naoochno-issledovatel'skiy instituot Voyennovozdooshnykh sil*, Red Banner State Air Force Research Institute) and the VVS itself indicated a top speed of 670 km/h at 7,000 m (23,000 ft). In addition, Romodin assessed a range of 784 km (486 miles) and an ability to climb to 5,000 m (16,400 ft) in 4.6 minutes and to 7,000 m (23,000 ft) in 6.8 minutes. A mock-up of the I-200 was approved on 25th December 1939 and all graphical drawings were completed by 10th February 1940.

Unfortunately, the AM-37 was not ready in time and the less powerful AM-35A, another supercharged V-12, which delivered only 1,200 hp (883 kW) at the same height, was substituted. The new engine also had a weight disadvantage, 830 kg (1,834 lb), particularly when compared with the Rolls-Royce Merlin (605 kg/1,334 lb) or the Klimov VK-105 (600 kg/1,323 lb). After meeting NKAP officials on 25th February 1940 to review progress, *zavod* No.1 and its OKO received new instructions from the Sovnarkom (*Sovet narodnykh komissarov*, Council of People's Commissars), on 4th March 1940. Echoed the next day by the NKAP, the new remit was to build three prototypes and prepare the factory for series production of the new interceptor which, because of its less powerful engine, would have a reduced top speed of 640 km/h (397 mph) at 7,000 m (23,000ft). It was common practice in the USSR to start preparations for mass production of a new aircraft before the prototype had flown but in this case it was also a blind act of faith in a new design team, which had yet to build an aircraft. It was undoubtedly the prestige of *zavod* No.1 that reassured the authorities; it was the most up-to-date aircraft factory in the country and the pride of the industry.

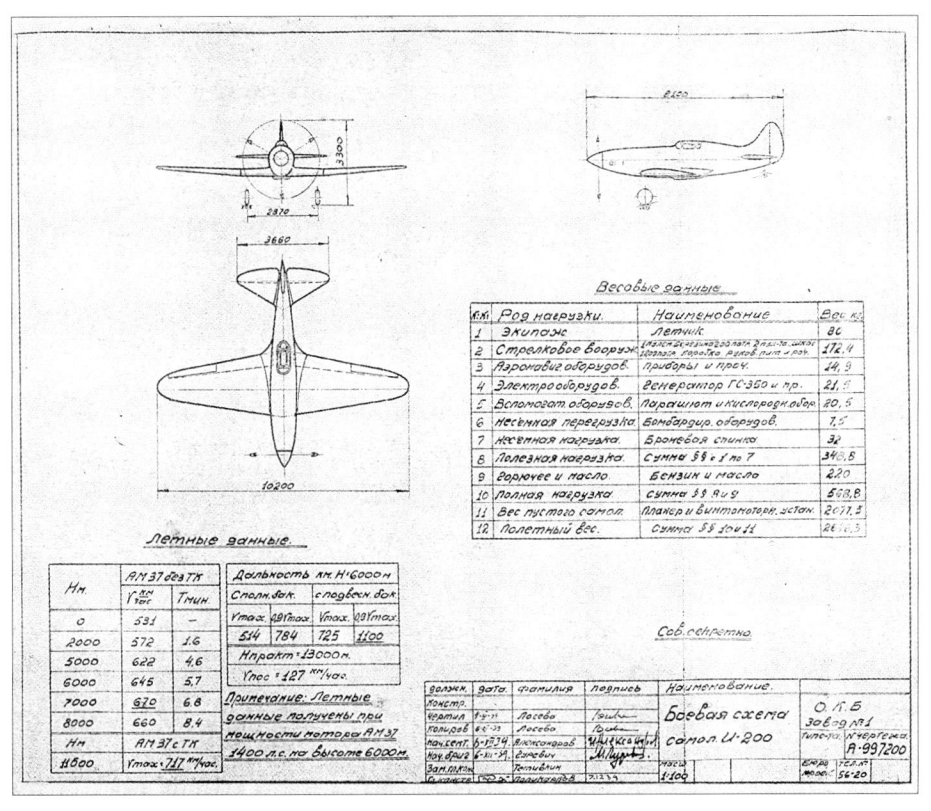

A schematic three-view and data table from the I-200's advanced development project documents.

The I-200 was a sleek low-wing monoplane characterised by a cockpit positioned well aft in the manner of the racing aircraft of the day. One of the design objectives was to produce the smallest possible airframe. Although another was to minimise the use of lightweight metals, these were in such short supply that construction, by necessity, had to be mostly of wood. However, the wing centre section was an all-metal structure with an I-section single main spar made of 20KhGSA grade steel. The fuselage had a wooden rear section but the front section, from spinner to rear of cockpit, was composed of welded steel tubes covered by 12 duralumin skin panels secured by fasteners.

The wings were evenly tapered with rounded tips and the wooden outer wing panels had 5° dihedral. Both main and tail landing gear struts were retractable, the former folding inwards into the wing centre section. Retraction was performed pneumatically, a boon to pilots who had previously flown the I-16 with its manually operated retraction

Above and below: The first prototype of the I-200 fighter (c/n 01) seen during manufacturer's flight tests. The aircraft was painted silver overall, with a red lightning bolt down the side.

Above: Head-on view of the first prototype. The dihedral on the wooden outer wings is evident; the air intakes in the wing roots are for the engine inlet manifold.
Below: A curious feature of the first prototype was the flaps just aft of the spinner regulating the airflow through the oil coolers buried in the sides of the cowling.

Above and below: The second prototype I-200 (c/n 02) was painted a glossy light grey overall – and again devoid of national insignia. From this aircraft onwards the forward-mounted oil cooler doors were deleted, resulting in characteristic 'nostrils' on the sides of the cowling.

Front and rear views of the same aircraft. It is seen here at GK NII VVS airfield in Schcholkovo east of Moscow during State acceptance trials (note the characteristic hexagonal concrete slabs making up the hardstand).

Above and below: Three-quarters rear views of the second prototype I-200 during State acceptance trials. The flaps are fully deployed in the lower picture. Note the canopy retaining rod at the rear of the sideways-opening canopy – a design that was soon to change.

The second prototype I-200 trestled for landing gear retraction checks at GK NII VVS. Note the air bottle which supplied compressed air for the gear actuation cylinder when the engine was inoperative.

mechanism. An important feature of the design was its adaptation for mass production; sub-assemblies were diligently created for quick assembly.

The engine drove a VISh-22Ye three-blade variable pitch propeller 3.0 m (9 ft 10 in) in diameter. A large spinner was fitted and a ventral water radiator positioned well back almost under the cockpit. Air for the supercharger entered through two intakes in the wing roots and the oil cooler was placed on the port side of the nose. There were three exhaust pipes each side, with one for every two cylinders, an arrangement that augmented forward thrust.

On 31st March 1940 the unarmed prototype (construction number 01) was trundled round to the nearby Central Airfield and the first flight took place on 5th April with Factory Chief Test Pilot Arkadiy N. Yekatov at the controls. Ground support was supplied by A. G. Broonov, the chief engineer for the venture, with Colonel M. I. Martselyuk representing the VVS and Major M. N. Yakooshin the VVS Flight Inspection. The annual May Day flypast included the I-200, again with Yekatov as pilot. Amazingly, it passed unnoticed by Western observers. In a measure to speed up the State Acceptance programme, two more I-200s were quickly built: the second prototype (c/n 02), completed on 25th April, made its maiden flight on 9th May 1940, piloted by Yakooshin. However, when the third aircraft (c/n 03) started ground-based weapons tests on 13th May, the synchronisation gear was not yet fully operational. It did not become so until 1st June, delaying the initial flight until 6th June 1940 when M. I. Martselyuk flew it. No.03 differed from the first two prototypes in having all-metal outer wings and FS-155 landing lights replacing the NG-12 flare holders.

Formal instructions to start serious preparations for series production at *zavod* No.1 were given by NKAP on 31st May 1940 after getting the go-ahead from the *Komitet Oborony* (Defence Committee) on 25th May. The factory was pressed to assemble 125 I-200s and discontinue production of the Yakovlev BB-22 twin-engined light bomber.

Factory tests were initiated using the first two prototypes immediately after their first flights and were successfully completed on 25th August 1940 after 109 flights lasting a total of nearly 41 hours. On 24th May the first prototoype, flown by A. N. Yekatov, achieved a top speed of 648 km/h (402 mph) at 6,900 m (22,600 ft) without maximum boost. On 5th August M. N. Yakooshin attained 651 km/h (404 mph) at 7,000 m (23,000 ft), also without boosting. When employing maximum boost, records show a time of 5.1 minutes to 5,000 m (16,400 ft) and 7.2 minutes to 7,000 m (23,000 ft) with top speeds of 579 km/h (359 mph) at 2,220 m (7,300 ft) and 605 km/h (375 mph) at 3,630 m (11,900 ft).

M. N. Yakooshin flew I-200 c/n 01 in the flypast at the Air Force Day celebrations at Tushino, then a suburb of Moscow, on 18th August 1940 when a large crowd, including numerous prestigious foreign guests and journalists, watched the performance. On 29th August I-200s No.01 and No.02 joined the State acceptance trials which were successfully concluded on 12th September 1940.

There was a narrow escape for one of the prototypes on the last day of the trials when, immediately after take-off; engine failure obliged the pilot, Andrei Kochatov, to make a forced landing. He managed to land safely at the end of the runway in spite of running out of fuel in the selected tank at 200 m (650 ft). The origin of the problem was traced to poor design of the tank selector valve.

Whilst delight was expressed with the overall performance, it was admitted that the aircraft was extremely difficult to control for inexperienced pilots. During State acceptance trials Stepan P. Sooproon achieved a top speed of 651 km/h (404 mph) at 7,000 m (23,000 ft) and a time to 5,000 m (16,400 ft) of 5.3 minutes. A comparison with competitors indicated that the I-26 (later Yak-1) had a top speed of 586 km/h (363 mph) and time to 5,000 m of 6.0 minutes, the Lavochkin/

Above and below: The third prototype I-200 (c/n 03) was painted a glossy dark green with pale blue undersurfaces and again lacked any markings whatsoever. It also lacked the hinged canopy section and the upper view shows the dished seat pan. The lower photo was taken at GK NII VVS during State acceptance trials.

Gorboonov/Goodkov I-301 (later LaGG-1) had 375 mph (605 km/h) and 5.85 minutes, and the I-180-3 showed 357 mph (575 km/h) and 5.8 minutes. Although these aircraft had different roles and were not directly comparable, they do show why the VVS was so keen to promote rapid production of the I-200. However, there were problems, including deficient forward visibility when taxying, generally poor visibility because of distortion, heavy controls, poor longitudinal stability, difficulty in opening the hood, overheating in the cabin – and, worst of all, a dangerous propensity to spin after a simple stall from which it was almost impossible to recover.

Whilst series production was to continue unabated, the following improvements were ordered to be made as soon as possible. In addition to the proposed armament of two 7.62-mm (.30-calibre) Shpital'nyy/Komaritskiy ShKAS machine-guns and one 12.7-mm (.50-calibre) Berezin UBS machine-gun in the nose synchronised to fire through the propeller, provision should be made for two detachable gun pods under the wings. Fuel capacity should be sufficient to give a range of at least 1,000 km (620 miles) at 90% of the top speed. Self-sealing fuel tanks were to be installed; the main undercarriage was to be brought up to NKAP standard and the solid tailwheel tyre replaced by a pneumatic one. Longitudinal and roll stability were to be improved, control forces reduced, leading-edge slats fitted and more effective oil cooling provided.

Such was the need for new fighter planes that most of the above improvements could not be immediately incorporated into the aircraft coming off the production lines. In fact, *wing slats were never fitted to either the MiG-1*. However, the following changes were able to be made to the MiG-1 specification before series production started. The ventral water radiator bath was extended further forward, and the single control flap in the radiator was replaced by a double flap. Rubber sheaths were placed round the fuel tanks to make them self-sealing. An additional oil cooler air intake was provided on the starboard side of the nose.

The hinged lower halves of the mainwheel doors were relocated onto the sides of the wheel wells. Two underwing hardpoints were introduced for carrying either two 50-kg (110-lb) FAB-50 or two 100-kg (220-lb) FAB-100 bombs. A PBP-1 gunsight was fitted; the two ShKAS machine-guns were given 375 rounds per gun and the UBS machine-gun 300 rounds. From the ninth production aircraft onwards, an aft-sliding cockpit canopy which could be jettisoned in the event of an emergency replaced the sideways-hinged type.

As a result of a recent decision by Stalin, the I-200 was redesignated MiG-1 on 9th

Above: This view of I-200 c/n 02 shows that the port and starboard oil cooler intakes were shaped differently to maximise their efficiency, making use of the airflow organisation around the nose.

Above: From I-200 c/n 02 onwards the oil cooler tunnels featured aft-mounted airflow regulator flaps. Note the oblong steel strip aft of the exhaust stubs protecting the duralumin skin from the hot exhaust.

The nose of the second prototype with some of the cowling panels removed.

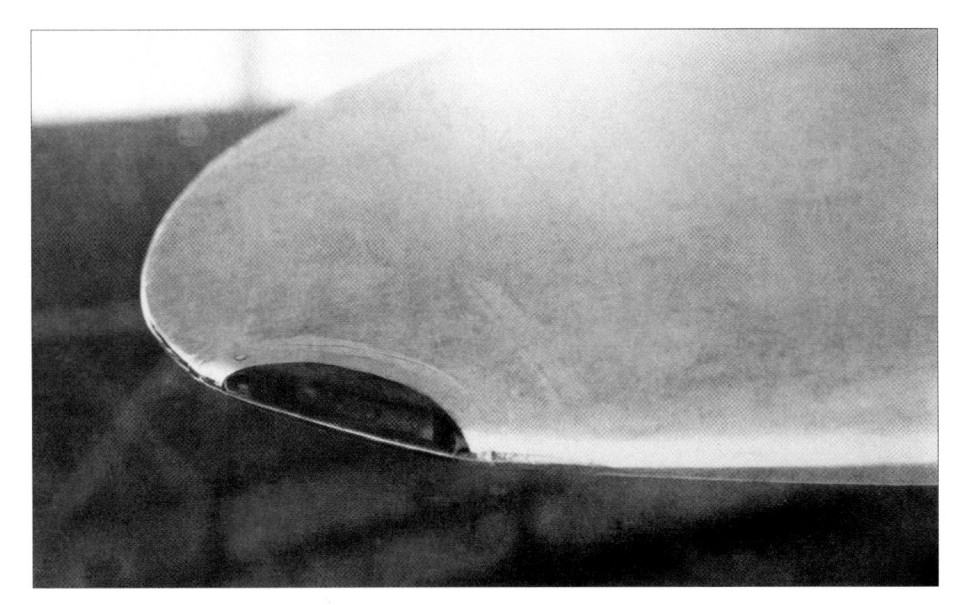

Above: The starboard navigation light of an I-200.

Above: The open cowling of an I-200 shows the firewall and the breeches of the machine-guns.

Another view through the removed upper part of the engine cowling, showing the barrels of the two synchronised ShKAS (left and right) machine-guns and the heavy UBS machine-gun in the middle.

December 1940. Service aircraft, as distinct from prototypes, were to be designated with the initials of the designer followed by even numbers for bombers and odd numbers for fighters, hence the next fighter from the OKO was MiG-3.

Towards the end of 1939 the military asked the OKO to modify the design of the MiG-1 to enable ten 82-mm RS-82 unguided rockets to be carried under the wings. After preliminary discussions on 13th April 1940, GK NII VVS recommended using eight RS-82 rockets and it was agreed to try this combination on the second prototype, as formalised in a decree of the Chief Military Council of the Red Army (Glavnyy Voennyy Sovet Krasnoy Armii) on 28th May 1940. In the meantime the NKAP had authorised work to be started and asked for additional wing protection in the shape of bolted-on duralumin panels to cover the leading edge and undersurfraces between rib Nos. 1 to 6. Subsequently, it transpired that the panels were unnecessary and were not fitted to production aircraft. It was originally intended that 10% of all production would be delivered with rocket launch rails already installed; however, on 14th February 1941 NKAP rescinded the order but reinstated it again on the 24th September. Trials carried out on the third prototype subsequently revealed that the optimum number of rockets carried should be reduced to six.

Exactly 100 MiG-1 aircraft had been built by mid-December 1940, by which time a sufficient number of improvements had been incorporated on the production lines to merit a change of designation to MiG-3.

On 3rd December the VVS decreed that the 41st IAP (*istrebitel'nyy aviatsionnyy polk*, fighter aviation regiment) at Kacha on the Crimea Peninsula should be the operational trials centre for the MiG-1 and continue to be so until February 1941. On 4th December NKAP instructed the director of *zavod* No.1 to despatch 10 MiG-1s to the 41st IAP by 15th December and ordered that Stepan P. Sooproon be put in charge of the trials which would also determine battle tactics. Furthermore, three MiG-1s were to go to GK NII VVS for more military trials. After completion of the trials the aircraft were to be flown to the 146th IAP at Yevpatoria for pilot training.

At the beginning of 1940, first-line regiments began to receive MiG-1s. By 22nd February 1941 a total of 89 had been delivered to the 31st IAP at Kovno, Baltic Defence District, and to the 41st IAP at Belostok, Western Defence District. The other eleven were dispersed as follows: three were at test facilities awaiting delivery, three were being dismantled prior to packing in crates, three more were undergoing various specific tests, one was awaiting its factory tests and the last one was not quite finished.

As with many types, the MiG-1 suffered appreciable losses in the first few days of the German invasion which began in the early hours of 22nd June 1941 when German bombers attacked Soviet airfields. Surprisingly, at least one survived until 1944 when it was recorded in VVS records as having been removed from the inventory that year.

MiG-1 with AM-37 engine

Perhaps it would be more accurate to refer to this experimental aircraft as the I-200 with an AM-37 engine. It was the second prototype I-200 (c/n 02) modified at the end of 1940 when an example of the new engine became available. Test pilot A. I. Zhookov made the first flight on 6th January 1941 and in the course of the factory test flights the engine ran irregularly and vibrated above 4,000 m (13,100 ft). After the intervention of P. V. Derment'yev the aircraft was sent on 26th April 1941 to *zavod* No.24 named after Mikhail V. Frunze in Moscow for remedial work on the engine. Flight tests continued but on 7th May, with I. T. Ivashchenko at the controls, engine failure resulted in a crash which destroyed the aircraft. Fortunately, the pilot survived.

IP-201

In an effort to improve the armament of the MiG-1, the third prototype I-200 was at first intended to receive two type MP-3 (PTB-23) 23 mm cannon under the wings, each with 60 rounds, in addition to retaining two ShKAS 7.62-mm machine-guns. The BS 12.7-mm machine-gun was omitted to make way for an extra 195-litre (42.9-Imp. gal.) fuel tank. Yakov G.Taubin and M. N. Baboorin had designed the cannon at OKB-16 of NKV (*Narkomat vo'oruzheniya*, People's Commissariat for Weapons) located in Moscow. Contained in streamlined underwing fairings, the cannon fired outside the propeller's arc. Under overload conditions it was also possible to carry two 100-kg (220-lb) bombs.

Extra drag from the cannon pods reduced top speed by 15 km/h (9.3 mph), but as the I-200's top speed had been recorded at about 650 km/h (403 mph) the reduction was considered acceptable. A working mock-up of the cannon in the left wing was demonstrated at three factories and on 27th July 1940 an NKAP committee headed by B. N. Yur'ev convened to consider the project. However, new calculations suggested the top speed would fall even further to an unacceptable 615 km/h (382 mph). Furthermore, GK NII VVS became involved and on 14th August voiced concern at the cannons' rate of fire – a mere 300 rounds per minute. Nonetheless, towards the end of September work started on modifying I-200 c/n 03 and the aircraft was sent from GK NII VVS to *zavod* No.1 to rectify any defects before installation of the cannon.

Above: The starboard cockpit console of the I-200 featuring circuit breakers, a rotating bomb selector knob below them, a clock, a voltmeter and a fuse box.

Above: The main instrument panel with a PBP-1 gunsight (featuring a padded chin rest) above it.

The RSI-3 radio set installed beneath the rear portion of the canopy.

The port cockpit console featuring the throttle (with the boost control lever immediately below), the flap and undercarriage controls further down and the propeller pitch control wheel in the upper right corner.

Agreement was formally given on 12th October 1940 by NKAP to NKV allowing the replacement of two ShKAS machine-guns by two 23-mm MP-3 cannon on the I-200. Pressure was brought to bear on the cannon's designers to increase the rate of fire and OKB-16 duly increased it to 600 rounds per minute; the improved cannon was redesignated MP-6. The authorities were delighted with this doubling of the rate of fire and on 16th November the Sovnarkom accepted the weapon. Instructions were given on 23rd November by NKAP and the VVS to the Mikoyan, Lavochkin, Il'yushin and Sukhoi design bureaux that within two months the MP-6 cannon and AP-12.7 machine-guns were to be used in their aircraft. As a result, the IP-201 project (*istrebitel' pushechnyy* – cannon-armed fighter) proceeded with an armament of two 23-mm MP-6 cannon and two 12.7-mm AP-12.7 machine-guns. Taubin and Barbarin had persuaded some very influential people to instruct all leading designers of fighter and ground attack aircraft to use their guns.

Installation of the guns was difficult and when first attempted the wings deformed. Progress was further hampered when work on modifying I-200 No.03 had to stop for it to be restored to flying condition. Along with the first two I-200 prototypes it flew in an air parade over Red Square on 7th November 1940. With the installation of the cannon completed, the first and, as it turned out, only flight thus armed was carried out by V. N. Goorskiy on 1st December 1940. Unfortunately, a forced landing had to be made because of a blockage in the fuel line from the fuselage tank. The performance of both types of guns proved, after many trials on other aircraft, to be very unsatisfactory and a decision was made to terminate the experiment. Both NKAP and the VVS had expressed high hopes of the new guns, and their loss of face in recommending their use so highly demanded retribution. On 15th May 1941 the hapless Taubin and Baboorin were placed under arrest and executed on 28th October 1941. The IP-201 was repaired by February 1941 but returned to its former configuration as I-200 No.03.

Structural description of the MiG-1

Aware of the shortage of duralumin and special steels, the OKO designed the MiG-1 with a traditional Soviet mixed wood and metal construction with the centre, forward fuselage and wing centre section having a metal framework whilst that of the outer wings and rear fuselage was wooden. The entire forward fuselage from the spinner to the back of the cockpit had a framework of welded 30KhGSA grade stainless steel tubes of oval cross section and a tensile strength of 110 kg/mm^2; this framework also formed a cradle for the engine. To secure the heavy engine of 830 kg (1,830 lb) the tubular cradle was pin-jointed to the front ends of the upper longerons of the centre fuselage and to the noses of the wing-root ribs by diagonal compression struts. Great care was taken to ensure that the duralumin panels enclosing the engine were shaped to minimise drag.

Behind the engine was the short centre fuselage of which the front members were bolted onto the top of the main spar and with its backwards sloping rear members situated immediately behind the pilot's seat. The four main longitudinal tubes were 40 x 36 mm (1.575 x 1.417 in) and the others either 30 x 27 mm (1.181 x 1.062 in) or 25 x 22 mm (0.984 x 0.866 in). The guns rested on bosses attached to another two longitudinal tubes at the front of this section. Twelve duralumin skin panels covered the tubular structure and were secured by Dzus quick-release fasteners. The rear section was a semi-monocoque all-wood structure integral with the tailfin, featuring four pine longerons attached to the corresponding centre section tubes ending in S-20A steel forgings machined to form bolted joints. In addition to these longerons there were eight hollow frames with a Bakelite-ply web, pine stringers and gusset plates also of Bakelite ply under the attachment points. The entire rear section was covered in an outer skin of Bakelite ply.

Shpon was a type of plywood made from strips of birch wood bonded together with casein glue, each strip placed at right angles to the next for extra strength. Bakelite ply consisted of layers of 0.5-mm (0.19-in) *shpon*, usually five, each layer built up from narrow diagonal strips placed over a former to give the shape required before the next layer was attached to it, using *mitkal'* (calico) strips impregnated with a nitro-cellulose varnish on one side and bonded with casein glue; the skin was pinned to maintain its shape. When completed the carcass was fitted round the structural elements and glued into place whilst held in a steel jig in which closely positioned screw presses were hand-adjusted to force the skin down on to the appropriate member. After the external surfaces had set, their holes and crevices were covered with a nitro-filling before being coated with nitro-cellulose glue onto which calico was affixed. The inside surfaces were given a protective coat of AKh-9 grey enamel paint.

Four 6-mm (0.23-in) steel bolts spaced 60 mm (2.3 in) apart attached the all-metal wing centre section structure to the fuselage. An I-shaped wing centre section spar had flanges made of 20KhGSA grade stainless steel and a web of two 2-mm (0.08-in) thick light alloy sheets stiffened by riveted vertical angles. Each of these angles had upper and lower L-pieces of heat-treated 20KhGSA and forked joints with the outer wing. The span of the centre section was 2.8 m (9 ft 2¼ in) with the main spar positioned at 45% chord. Two shorter auxiliary spars, one each side of the main spar, plus five formers held the flush riveted duralumin skin. Thirteen duralumin ribs, of which two were reinforced at the wing roots, completed the structure; each root rib had a forward extension to carry an attachment to the lower engine mount.

The wings had an aspect ratio of 5.97, a Clark YH aerofoil section and a thickness/chord ratio of 14% at the root decreasing to 8% at the tip. They tapered sharply away from the roots and as the lower surface was flat, the upper had a slight anhedral. Below the centre section the duralumin skin was held by flush rivets, which wrapped around the leading edge. On each side, between the main and

Above: I-200 c/n 02 levelled for boresighting the machine-guns. Note the hinged portions of the main gear doors reflecting the fighter's Polikarpov heritage.
Below: The same aircraft prepared for spin tests. The hinged portion of the canopy has been removed to facilitate baling out, should recovery prove impossible.

Секретно.

rear auxiliary spar, there was a 150-litre (33-Imp. gal.) fuel tank. A removable stiffened panel, attached at 60-mm (2.3-in) intervals with 6-mm (0.23-in) countersunk bolts screwed into nuts in the wing structure, was fitted under each fuel tank. The inboard flaps and main undercarriage were also contained in the wing centre section.

The outer wings with 5° dihedral had single-spar wooden panels tapered to a rounded, slightly pointed, tip. The box-type spar had a web of seven 4-mm (0.15-in) plywood sheets at the inboard end, reducing to five at the wingtips. The 14-15 mm gap filled with *del'ta-drevesina* (compressed wood impregnated with formaldehyde resin) formed a flange. From 115 mm (4½ in) wide the spar box tapered down to 75 mm (3 in) at the wingtips. Auxiliary spars of pine plywood were each attached to their opposite number in the centre section by a horizontal bolt but the important joint between the main spars had a fitting of laminated steel secured by two 12-mm (½-in) diameter bolts of high-tensile steel. The ribs in the outer wings were wooden with vertical stiffeners and ply sheet webs on both sides for rib Nos. 1-5 but only on the outer side for ribs from No.6 onwards. A panel of Bakelite-ply skin having five layers ranging in thickness from 2.5 to 4.0 mm (0.09 to 0.15 in) bonded with casein glue, covered the leading edge and was attached to the top and bottom of the front spar. Stringers between the main spar and its two auxiliaries supported the diagonally applied Bakelite-ply skin on the remainder of the wing.

Schrenk-type (split) all-metal flaps were fitted: one on the centre section and another on the outer panel of each wing, making four in all. Constructed from D16 duralumin with riveted channel section reinforcements on the top surfaces, they were pneumatically operated with two settings, 18° for take-off and 50° for landing. Frise-type ailerons on the outer wing panels were covered with AST-100 fabric over D16 duralumin frames and leading edges. Each aileron had two sections joined by a two-axis universal joint upon which there was a projection for the centre bearing of the aft auxiliary wing spar.

The horizontal tail had an area 18% that of the wings and consisted of two D16 duralumin spars supported between eleven sheet metal ribs punched with flanged holes to reduce weight. Double strips, top and bottom, were attached by countersunk screws to both spars and a flush riveted skin attached. This was the only example on the aircraft of stressed-skin design. A three-fork forging secured each tailplane with a single bolt to the appropriate girder bridge piece, which in turn was joined by four bolts to the rear fuselage. The elevators had a similar construction to the ailerons but featured inset hinges.

A wooden vertical tail fin having a surface 8.75% of the wing area was integrated into the rear wooden fuselage. However, the rudder, like the elevators, had a D16 duralumin frame with perforated sheet ribs braced with D-16 tape. The upper part of the rudder was fabric covered, the lower had a metal skin. Inset hinges were utilised and a screw-actuated trim tab was made of AMTs aluminium.

On the three prototypes and first eight production aircraft the cockpit had a curved Plexiglas windscreen followed by a three-section one-piece hood hinged on the starboard side to facilitate pilot access. A fixed part of the hood extended behind the pilot and above a shelf on which an RSI-3 radio could be placed. From the ninth production aircraft a jettisonable canopy opened by sliding it backward on rollers replaced the hinged section. An aluminium bucket seat was provided with rubber-sprung struts and mechanisms for adjusting height and fore and aft position. The floor was constructed from sheet duralumin, pressed to shape and secured by three bolts. Rod-operated elevators and ailerons were linked to the control column, with a damping weight for the elevators, and cables connected the pedal-operated rudder. A Bowden cable controlled trim.

Instrumentation was minimal, featuring only 16 components in the cockpit: altimeter, NI-10 compass read-out, AG-1 artificial horizon, manifold pressure gauge, fuel gauge, airspeed indicator, turn and slip indicator, vertical speed indicator, tachometer, oil pressure gauge, oil temperature read-out, fuel pressure gauge, ambient temperature and pressure indicators and two pneumatic pressure gauges. Cockpit illumination was provided for day and night use and power for the navigation lights was available up to 30 volts by the GS-350 generator; other equipment included a 12A-5 battery and a KPA-3bis oxygen supply system.

Provision was made on the MiG-1 for the carriage of two bombs, either 50-kg (110-lb) FAB-50s or 100-kg (220-lb) FAB-100s, on underwing hardpoints; three machine-guns were installed above the engine, one 7.62-mm ShKAS on either side and one 12.7-mm UBS between them, slightly offset to port. Both ShKAS machine-guns were fed from readily replaceable boxes located between the engine and the fuel tank, each holding 375 rounds. A box holding 300 rounds was positioned underneath the UBS and a PBP-1 optical gunsight was installed.

Each of the main undercarriage units had an hydraulic strut made of 30KhGSA steel (130-150 kg/mm^2) filled with dialcohol (70% glycerine, 30% alcohol), with a maximum stroke of 270 mm (10.6 in) and a pressure of 39 kg/cm^2 (573 lb/sq.in). The brake-equipped wheels had 600 x 180 mm (23.62 x 7.0 in) tyres with the brake drum carried on two tapered roller bearings. The brakes and the retraction mechanism were operated pneumatically at up to 50 ata (632 psi), using a storage bottle which was maintained at 150 ata (2,200 psi) by an engine-driven compressor. The undercarriage track measured 2.8 m (9 ft 2¼ in) and the units retracted inwards into the wing centre section, the wheel well being sealed by a shaped plate attached to the strut and a D-shaped hinged plate fixed to the wheel well structure. The tailwheel, with a 170 x 90 mm (6.69 x 3.5 in) rubber tyre mounted on the forked end of a strut, swivelled about a pivot attached to a shock absorber. When the main gear retracted it was unlocked and retracted aft by cables, the gap under the centre section being closed by two doors. An electro-mechanical indicator on the instrument panel displayed landing gear position.

Derived from the AM-30 with its BMW VI type cylinder blocks, the 12-cylinder AM-35A was not the engine of choice; ideally, that was the undeveloped AM-37. Its reduction gear originated in the Rolls-Royce Buzzard and the single-stage single-speed supercharger was originally an Allison design. Specifically developed for the Petlyakov TB-7 heavy bomber, it ran at only 2,050 rpm for take-off. Weighing in at 830 kg (1,834 lb), weight was not its only handicap; it also lacked provision for a cannon to fire through the propeller hub. Rated at 1,350 hp (993 kW) for take-off, it produced 1,200 hp (883 kW) between 3,000 m (9,800 ft) and 6,000 m (19,700 ft). An oval inlet with filter was positioned in each wing root to feed the supercharger with air through curved aluminium pipes. Starting was activated pneumatically. Exhaust exited through six pipes made from EYa1-TL-1 heat-resistant steel, each pipe serving two cylinders. Oil cooler air inlets controlled by a hinged flap at the exit were located on either side of the engine and fed from a tank positioned above the reduction gear. Oil was cooled in a matrix just inside the duct, the amount of cooling controlled by the pilot adjusting the inlet flap.

Cooling of the engine was effected by undiluted glycol circulating in a 40-litre (8.8-Imp. gal.) unpressurised system through a wide honeycomb radiator with a frontal area of 0.23 m^2 (2.5 sq.ft). The radiator was positioned in a shallow duct mounted to the rear of the centreplane and controlled by pilot adjustment of the flap at the back of the duct. Compared with I-200, the duct was extended slightly forward and had been given a more aerodynamic shape.

The spinner was made of Elektron, a magnesium alloy, and the 3-m (9 ft 10-in) diameter VISh-22Ye propeller had three alloy blades adjusted by a hydraulically actuated constant speed unit over a range from 24° to 44°.

Chapter 2
Mikoyan Makes His Mark

The First Major Production Version

MiG-3 (I-200 No.04, *izdeliye* 61)

Throughout production of the MiG-1 in the last quarter of 1940, frantic efforts were made by the OKO of *zavod* No.1 to remedy its defects, and diagnostic tests were initiated on a full-scale aircraft in the enormous new T-1 wind tunnel at TsAGI (*Tsentrahl'nyy aeroghidrodinamicheskyy instittoot*, Central Aero- and Hydrodynamics Institute). As a result many changes were made, and introduced piecemeal onto the production lines.

The following alterations were made to the MiG-1 specification. The engine was set 100 mm (4 in) further forward to improve longitudinal stability. A new OP-310 water radiator having a deeper duct and an adjustable exit flap was fitted to give more efficient cooling. The above modifications created space for an extra 250-litre (55-Imp. gal.) petrol tank to be installed under the pilot's seat. A second oil tank was fitted beneath the engine.

To minimise the fire risk if hit by enemy fire, cooled engine exhaust gases were used to form an inert gas blanket in the fuel tanks. The back of the pilot's seat was armoured with an 8-mm (⁵⁄₁₆-in) or, on later aircraft, a 9-mm (¹¹⁄₃₂-in) plate.

The supercharger air intakes were streamlined. Longitudinal stability was further improved by increasing the dihedral of the outer wing panels by 1°. The main undercarriage was strengthened and larger 650 x 200 mm (25.5 x 7.87 in) tyres and brake drums used. To improve the rear view, the cockpit canopy glazing was extended aft and a shelf fitted behind the seat on which a radio could be installed when available. At first, RSI-1 single-channel receivers were installed but later were replaced by the RSI-4 model.

A more efficient VISh-61Sh propeller was fitted from the summer of 1941 and increased the pitch range to 35°.

In the cockpit, the PBP-1A gunsight replaced the PBP-1 and the instrument layout was improved and extended. The ammunition supply for the two ShKAS machine-guns was increased to 750 rounds per gun. The number of underwing hardpoints was doubled and a greater variety of armament permitted. Bombs from 8 to 100 kg (18 to 220 lb) could be carried up to a maximum of 220 kg (485 lb); alternatively, two VAP-6M or ZAP-6 spray containers for poison gas or incendiary fluids or eight unguided RS-82 rockets could be carried. In the event, the spray containers were never utilised in war.

All the above improvements were incorporated in the first prototype MiG-3. Its official designation (I-200 No.04) indicated that the aircraft was converted from the fourth prototype of the I-200 (c/n 04). Its first flight took place on 29th October 1940 with A. N. Yekatov as pilot. After factory trials the prototype went to GK NII VVS for State acceptance trials. The first production MiG-3 (construction number 2101) was completed on 20th December 1940. Up to the end of the year,

This aircraft, officially called I-200 No.4 (ie, c/n 04), was the prototype of the MiG-3.

Above and below: Two more views of the MiG-3 prototype (I-200 No.04). The redesigned cockpit canopy with sliding hood is visible, as are the redesigned main landing gear doors and the larger and deeper ventral radiator bath.

Front and rear views of the MiG-3 prototype during trials.

Above and below: A MiG-3 undergoing full-scale aerodynamic tests in TsAGI's T-101 wind tunnel on 8th March 1941. Note the test equipment sensors on the tail surfaces.

zavod No.1 assembled 20 MiG-3s, in addition to the 100 MiG-1s.

On 9th December 1940 NKAP outlined its 1941 production plan for the MiG-3. In accordance with it, zavod No.1 was to deliver 3,500 aircraft; zavod No.43 named after Maxim Gor'kiy in Kiev was to prepare for production and complete 100 MiG-3s by the end of the year (the German invasion and occupation of Kiev scuppered this plan). Finally, zavod No.21 named after Sergo Ordzhonikidze in Gor'kiy (now renamed back to Nizhniy Novgorod) was to start planning production of a developed version of the MiG-3; this order was rescinded shortly after.

The production output continued to rise until October 1941, by which time the advancing Germans were getting dangerously close to Moscow and it was considered judicious to evacuate the factory along with its OKO to Kuibyshev (now renamed back to Samara). There it absorbed zavod No.122, an aviation plant under construction and destined to produce MiG-3s.

State acceptance trials at GK NII VVS involving two production MiG-3s (c/ns 2107 and 2115) built in December 1940 took place between 27th January and 26th February 1941. In addition to establishing performance data and flying characteristics, comparisons were to be made with the MiG-1 to determine the effectiveness of the modifications made. The pilot in charge of the tests was Captain A. G. Proshakov to be assisted by an engineer, A. G. Kochetkov.

The tests gave disappointing results in comparison with the MiG-1s previously tested (see table at the end of this chapter). Weight was heavier by over 250 kg (550 lb), adversely affecting manoeuvrability and field performance. Climb to 5,000 m (16,400 ft) took over a minute longer; the service ceiling was 500 m (1,640 ft) lower. Fortunately top speed at sea level and altitude was higher than the MiG-1's. Crucially, the range was only 820 km (509 miles) for aircraft c/n 2115 and 857 km (531 miles) for c/n 2107 – both figures, although appreciably better than the MiG-1, were well below the 1,000 km (620 miles) demanded by the VVS. In the opinion of the GK NII VVS team the problem stemmed from the fact that the engine had a 10-15% greater specific fuel consumption (SFC) than the manufacturer, zavod No.24, had guaranteed; this difference, it was intimated, accounted for the failure to meet the NKAP target.

Artyom Mikoyan and Mikhail Gurevich were dismayed by the failure to achieve the desired range and wrote to Aleksey I. Shakhurin, the recently appointed head of NKAP, asserting that calculations predicted the range of the MiG-3 to be at least 1,010 km (626 miles) based on an SFC of 0.46 kg/km (1.64 lb/mile). During State acceptance trials

Above: The rear fuselage skin of a MiG-3 is secured to the internal structural members by numerous clamps during the bonding process.

Above: The rear fuselage could be rotated in the assembly jig like shish kebab on a spit. Note that the fin was manufactured integrally with the rear fuselage.

An assembly worker at work on the one-piece all-metal inner wing assembly. The main landing gear struts are already attached.

Above: The Mikulin AM-35 engine complete with engine bearer mounted on a work jig prior to installation in a MiG-3.

Above: Assembly of the MiG-3's cowling on a jig to make sure all panels fit as they should before they are fitted around the actual engine.

The fighter takes shape as the the centre fuselage truss housing the cockpit section is mated to the wing centre section; the main gear doors are already in place. The whole assembly rests on a transport dolly.

the SFC was 0.48 kg/km (1.71 lb/mile) but during the joint trials with GK NII VVS at Kacha the SFC was 0.38 kg/km (1.35 lb/mile). They emphatically attributed blame for the deficient range during State acceptance trials to the fact that an altitude correction had not been used and, in addition, there had been an incorrect adjustment of the engines.

To reinforce their allegation Mikoyan and Gurevich arranged two more test flights between Moscow and Leningrad in which an average unrefuelled range of 1,000 km was achieved. Two series-produced MiG-3s (construction numbers 2592 and 2597) performed the tests at 90% maximum speed and an altitude of 7,300 m (23,900 ft), the first fighter achieving 1,100 km (683 miles) and the second 970 km (601 miles). These results were a direct contradiction of the findings of GK NII VVS.

Complaints based on numerous reports of substandard aircraft received by regiments had already been levelled at the institute, which was responsible for monitoring the quality of aircraft delivered to the VVS. Examples included inefficiently harmonised machine-guns on MiG-3s. On 31st May 1941 the NKO (*Narodnyy komissariat oborony* – People's Comissariat of Defence) decreed that GK NII VVS had failed to sustain production quality; many senior managers were demoted but a worse fate awaited its director, Major General A. I. Filin, who was summarily executed.

After the MiG-3 entered service it was discovered that, although optimised for high altitude interception, the performance of some MiG-3s above 5,000 m (16,400 ft) was totally unacceptable. It was not much better above 3,000 m (9,800), the height at which both the fuel pump output and oil pressure started to fall. Oxygen supply equipment was also inefficient and there was still the problem of unacceptable stall and spin recovery characteristics. This situation became critical on 10th April 1941 after three pilots of the 31st IAP PVO (*Protivovozdooshnaya oborona* – Air Defence Force) attempted to attack German reconnaissance machines overflying Kaunas, Lithuania, at 9,000 m (29,500 ft). All three aircraft went into an irrecoverable spin; the pilots baled out but one was killed.

In order to locate and redress the problems A. G. Kochetkov, an engineer and pilot of GK NII VVS, was sent to the regiment's base at Kovno, near Kaunas. He discovered that the pilots, who had accrued very few flying hours on the type, compounded the aircraft's shortcomings and, worse still, it was their first high-altitude sortie. The recommendations included:

better training;

more explicit guidance, which was then but outlined, on the safe handling of the aircraft at high altitudes – particularly with regard to how to safely perform combat manoeuvres without spinning;

installation of automatic mixture controls on the carburettors;

modification to the oil system to maintain oil pressure;

fitting fuel pumps which would operate effectively at up to 11,000 m (36,000 ft).

With a pair of 7.62-mm ShKAS machine-guns and one 12.7-mm UBS machine-gun, the MiG-3 was lightly armed by the standards of 1941. In contrast, the majority of Messerschmitt Bf 109 variants in use on the Eastern Front had at least one 20-mm MG FF cannon and two 7.62-mm MG 17 machine-guns. Of the 3,172 MiG-3s built, more than half (1,976) had the standard armament, but in mid-1941 821 aircraft were supplemented with one 12.7-mm Berezin BK machine-gun in a removable gondola under each wing. The weight of fire was thereby increased from 1.38 kg (3.1 lb) to 3.0 kg (6.6 lb) per second. Unfortunately the aircraft's performance deteriorated drastically, top speed dropping by about 20 km/h (12 mph) at all altitudes. In some instances, regiments reduced the amount of fuel carried in an attempt to recoup the loss; many others simply removed the gun pods. Other combinations were tried and three MiG-3s were given two UBS' and one ShKAS. Two more aircraft had a pair of ShKAS' and one UBS supplemented by two 3ROB-82 rocket launchers, each carrying three RO-82 unguided rockets.

As recounted earlier, the military were keen to receive aircraft with rocket launchers and these two aircraft continued the earlier experiments with I-200 c/n 03. Instead of individual racks the MiG-3s were fitted with 2ROB-82 or 3ROB-82B launchers for two or three rockets respectively. This modification facilitated installation and re-arming as the fittings were reduced to two brackets per mounting instead of six. Later the simplified URO-82 replaced the ROB-82 type racks. In the field the intended type of rocket was not always available and special wing-mounted circuits were added to extend use to a wide variety of rockets on air-to-ground missions; eg, 82-mm RO-82s, RO-82Ms and URO-82s or 132-mm RO-132s and RO-132Ms. Sighting for firing was to be by means of the PBP-1A gunsight but it was found preferable to paint a special grid on the windscreen. The pilot fired the rockets using an ESBR-3 electrically operated release unit on his port console.

It was originally intended to use the RO-82 rockets in aerial dogfights; to this end the rockets would be fitted with AGTD-A-RS-82 time-delay fuses, the delay (2 to 22 seconds) being set by the armourer. Until the German pilots learned effective evasive tactics the rockets scored some successes. Neverthe-

Above: More 'shish-kebab', this time the rear fuselage internal structure before the fastening of the skin. The way the rearmost fuselage formers and stringers blend into the fin spars/ribs is well illustrated.

Above: As the rear fuselage is fixed in another jig, a worker installs the lugs by which the assembly is mated with the centre fuselage truss.

The rear fuselage/fin assembly, complete with tailwheel strut, is painted and ready for mating with the rest of the airframe. Note the last two digits of the c/n (2109?) chalked on the fin.

Above and below: MiG-3 c/n 2115 seen during State acceptance trials in February 1941. The aircraft wears the typical camouflage of early-production MiG-3s with uniformly dark green upper surfaces and pale blue undersurfaces. Note the external stores hardpoints in the upper photo.

Above and below: Two more views of MiG-3 c/n 2115 at GK NII VVS. The last two digits of the c/n are crudely painted on the tail.

Above: This production MiG-3 is noteworthy for its light-coloured vertical tail and spinner tip which may be unit markings.

Above and below: The cockpit of a standard MiG-3. The curved transverse tube carrying the gunsight is part of the centre fuselage truss.

less, there was a desperate need to stop the advancing Wehrmacht and, in desperation, even high-altitude interceptors were pressed into service for air to ground attacks. In this role rockets with AM-A-RS-82 contact detonators were used which were not renowned for their accuracy and it was customary for the pilot, when attacking, to fire all rockets at once either in a salvo or in quick succession. The effective range was 800 m (2,600 ft) to 1,000 m (3,300 ft) compared with up to 200 m (650 ft) for machine-guns and 600 m (2,000 ft) for cannon.

A further 100 MiG-3s received just two 12.7-mm UBS machine-guns and another 215 with the same gun armament also had the two rocket launchers for six unguided rockets. A further 52 MiG-3s had two synchronised 20- mm ShVAK cannon in response to a study conducted with NII-13 and *zavod* No.235 in Votkinsk to discover the most suitable cannon and synchronising gear for a fighter aircraft. Testing of the cannon took place with MiG-3 c/n 6005. Three MiG-3s were built with no guns, one for TsAGI and the other two presumably for photographic reconnaissance work. The numbers given above of MiG-3s manufactured with the various gun armament options apply only to newly built aircraft. Many more, no doubt, were given other combinations of machine-guns and cannon in regimental workshops, either at the request of their pilots or because of a shortage of standard replacements.

Improvements were made to standard specifications in the course of production. For example, in the second half of 1941 the engine's reduction gear ratio was changed from 0.903 to 0.732 and the VISh-22Ye propeller replaced by the AV-5L-123 which had a greater range of pitch angles. Inevitably, most changes to the MiG-3 increased its weight with a corresponding deterioration in performance and manoeuvrability. At first the aircraft was left in a natural metal finish but later painting in camouflage colours exacerbated the weight problem.

Some concern had been expressed at the high landing speed of 144 km/h (89 mph) and in August 1941 TsAGI suggested that the fitting of trapezoidal wingtip fairings would reduce it by 4-5 km/h (2.5-3.0 mph) and also allow the span of the airbrakes to be increased. This was not implemented for two reasons: firstly, the amount of speed reduction was smaller than the error in measuring speed; secondly, the necessary changes to the production line to accommodate the changes would cause unacceptable losses of aircraft output.

On 20th December 1940 *zavod* No.1 started assembling MiG-3s; by the end of the year 20 had been built. During 1941 the production rate increased month by month: 140 in January, 496 in July, 562 in August and 450 in

September. By June 1941 *zavod* No.1 was turning out MiG-3s at a rate of 15 per day while *zavod* No.21 was building six LaGG-3s per day and *zavod* No.292 in Saratov only four Yak-1s. Of course direct comparisons should not be made, as there was no allowance made for the length of time the other two factories had been building the types specified; nonetheless it does indicate why *zavod* No.1 was held in high esteem.

By a superhuman effort, in a bleak Russian winter *zavod* No.1 was evacuated in October 1941 to Kuibyshev where production resumed. Output rate was building up again when the famous telegram was sent by Stalin in December 1941 to factory directors Shenkman (at *zavod* No.18) and Tret'yakov (at *zavod* No.1) complaining that the production rates of the Il'yushin IL-2 ground attack aircraft and the MiG-3 were derisory, adding that the IL-2 was '*as essential to our Red Army as air and bread*' and going on to say '*Let this be a last warning to you both*'. One result of this threat was that the AM-38 engine of the IL-2, which was built by the same factory as the MiG-3's AM-35A, was given absolute production priority. The supply of AM-35As dried up – and the IL-2 replaced the MiG-3 on the production lines at *zavod* No.1.

There is, however, some evidence that it always had been the intention of the government gradually to replace the MiG-3 at *zavod* No.1 with the IL-2. NKAP order No.921ss of 27th August 1941 gave instructions that 420 MiG-3 should be built at *zavod* No.1 in September, steadily declining to 100 in December by which time IL-2 production was planned to reach 250. A twin plant at Moscow-Khodynka was intended to build MiG-3s, but never did. This factory originated as the **A**viare**mont**nyy *zavod* No.1 (aircraft repair plant) of the UVVS (*Oopravleniye Voyenno-vozdooshnykh sil*, Air Force Directorate) and had become *zavod* No.165 on transfer to NKAP. The advance of the Wehrmacht towards Moscow resulted in the evacuation of factories to a safe haven further east, which threw these plans into disarray. Undoubtedly the disappointing performance of series-built products and the high accident rate of the MiG-3 contributed to the decision to terminate its production.

Of the 3,172 MiG-3 fighters built, 30 were completed in 1942, having been assembled with two 20-mm (.78-calibre) Shpital'nyy/ Vladimirov ShVAK cannon in a special facility created by Mikoyan at OKB-155. Component parts for 1942 production had been obtained from *zavod* No.1 in Kuybyshev and *zavod* No.30, which had recently been formed on the evacuated Khodynka site. Two MiG-3s then being overhauled at the plant were similarly equipped. We know that a further 20 newly built MiG-3s also received these cannon as it is recorded that the total given can-

Above: The port tailplane of a MiG-3. The difference in surface finish between the all-metal stabiliser and the fabric-covered elevator is obvious.

Inboard view of the port main gear unit. Note the holes around the wheel rim for brake cooling.

Above and below: MiG-3 c/n 2109 was one of several equipped with Berezin BK machine-guns in underwing pods. It is pictured here during tests held to determine how the gun pods affected the fighter's spinning characteristics.

Above: An in-service MiG-3 with podded BK machine-guns. Note the compressed-air bottle used for engine starting.
Below: A MiG-3 carrying BAS-1 bomblet/incendiary ampoule pods on the wing hardpoints. This experimental weapon was tested in mid-1941.

This photo taken on 30th August 1941 shows a MiG-3 with a retractable ski landing gear in TsAGI's T-101 wind tunnel; the tips of the retracted skis are just visible ahead of the wing roots. Note the airflow visualisation tufts all over the airframe and the non-standard extended trapezoidal wingtips.

non was 72; some sources suggest that the number assembled at OKB-155 was 50.

Throughout its service life the MiG-3 remained a very difficult aircraft to fly but its greatest problem was that the role for which it was designed, high-altitude interception, had appreciably diminished. Most of the air action at the front line took place below 5,000 m (16,400 ft) where the MiG-3 was outclassed not only by enemy but also by other Soviet fighters, the result being that many were sent to the PVO where their good high-altitude performance could be better employed. The MiG-3 was in fact used in the air defence of Moscow both in daylight and at night throughout most of the war. It had the advantage of being easy to maintain and repair and a reputation for being sturdily built, and in spite of production stopping at the end of 1941 some remained in service until the end of the war.

Basic Specifications of the I-200 (MiG-1) and MiG-3

Note that no data for the MiG-1 is shown as State acceptance trials were only carried out on the I-200 prototypes and not on production aircraft of this type.

Type	I-200	MiG-3	MiG-3	MiG-3
Construction Number	01 & 02	2107 & 2115	3839	3595
Test	State	State	NII VVS	NII VVS
Engine	AM-35A	AM-35A	AM-35A	AM-38
Rated output at take-off, hp (kW)	1,350 (993)	1,350 (993)	1,350 (993)	1,600 (1,178)
Reduction gear ratio	0.902	0.902	0.732	0.732
Propeller	VISh-22Ye	VISh-2Ye	AV-5L-23	AV-5L-110A
Span	10.2 m (33 ft 6 in)	10.2 m (33 ft 6 in)	10.2 m (33 ft 6 in)	10.2 m (33 ft 6 in)
Length	8.15 m (26 ft 9 in)	8.25 m (27 ft 1 in)	8.25 m (27 ft 1 in)	8.25 m (27 ft 1 in)
Wing area, m^2 (sq.ft)	17.44 (188)	17.44 (188)	17.44 (188)	17.44 (188)
Empty weight, kg (lb)	2,411 (5,328)	2,699 (5,965)	n.a.	2,780 (6,144)
Take-off weight, kg (lb)	3,099 (6,832)	3,355 (7,415)	3,299 (7,291)	3,325 (7,348)
Wing loading, kg/m^2 (lb/sq.ft)	178 (36.4)	192 (39.4)	189 (38.8)	191 (39.1)
Top speed at sea level, km/h (mph)	486 (301)	495 (307)	472 (293)	547 (339)
Top speed	636 (394)*	640 (397)	621 (385)	592 (367)
at altitude, m (ft)	7,600 (24,900)	7,800 (25,600)	7,800 (25,600)	3,400 (11,200)
Climb to 5,000m (16,400 ft), minutes	5.3	6.5	7.1	5.8
Service ceiling, m (ft)	12,000 (39,400)	11,500 (37,700)	11,500 (37,700)	9,500 (31,200)
Range, km (miles)	580 (360)	820 (508)	n.a.	n.a.
Take-off run, m (ft)	268 (879)	347 (1,138)	390 (1,279)	380 (1,246)
Landing run, m (ft)	400 (1,312)	410 (1,345)		400 (1,312)

* Originally assessed at 628 km/h (389 mph); later corrected to 636 km/h (394 mph)

Chapter 3

The MiG-3 in Action

A small batch of ten MiG-3s was sent in February 1941 to the Military Pilot School at Kacha in the Crimea to join the MiG-1s already there. Taking advantage of the warmer climate, more tests were conducted but tragically on 13th March 1941 during a flight by A. N. Yekatov in a MiG-3 (c/n 2147), the supercharger impeller disintegrated at high altitude, killing the pilot.

Two types of organisation existed at the outbreak of the Second World War for the defence of the USSR against enemy aircraft: the interceptor aircraft regiments of the VVS and the artillery, machine-gun and searchlight regiments of the Army. Both belonged theoretically to the *Oopravleniye protivovozdooshnoy oborony* (PVO Directorate) but operational control was firmly in the hands of local Military Districts or Fronts. The VVS Commander therefore controlled aircraft while the Army Commander of the Military District directed ground units. Co-ordination between the two organisations was, to say the least, haphazard

Fighter units defending the key areas around Moscow, Leningrad and Baku were grouped into three corps. Moscow was defended by the 6th IAK (*istrebitel'nyy aviatsionnyy korpoos*, Fighter aviation corps) formed on 20th June 1941. A little later, on 7th July, the 7th IAK was created for the defence of Leningrad, followed in November by the 8th IAK for Baku. Other cities were defended by smaller PVO components according to their size. The interceptor units were located in PVO Zones, as were anti-aircraft artillery and searchlight organisations. In August 1941 these PVO Zones were abolished, all constituents now reporting to the Commanders of the respective Fronts.

A first step in the integration of aircraft and Army PVO units took place on 9th November 1941 when PVO Corps Regions were created for Moscow and Leningrad (Baku followed later) and PVO Divisional Regions, PVO Divisional Zones and PVO Zones for other areas in descending order of size and importance. Prising the fighter regiments from the hard-pressed frontal units took some time but on 22nd January 1942, by order of the NKO, all fighter units attached to the PVO *Strany* (PVO of the Country) came under the control of Commander-in-Chief of the National Air Defence Forces (*Komanduyushchiy voysk PVO strany*). Effectively the PVO, like the Army, Navy and Air Force, had become a separate arm of the Soviet Armed Forces.

On 20th June 1941 the PVO possessed 40 fighter regiments with a total of 1,500 aircraft of which the 6th IAK had 387, including 175 of modern design. The MiG-3 was an ideal aircraft for the PVO and by the end of July the aircraft establishment of the 6th IAK had risen to 495 interceptors, of which there were 127 MiG-3s, 37 LaGG-3s and 91 Yak-1s plus 170 I-16s and 70 I-153s. Thus 255 (over 50%) were modern designs. Around Moscow 11 fighter regiments (plus two just forming, as yet with no aircraft) and two detachments were deployed. Listed below are the units equipped at that time with MiG-3 fighters although no regiment was exclusively provided with them. The data comes from the book *Neizvestnaya bitva v nebe Moskvy 1941-42* (The Unknown Battle in Moscow Skies 1941-42) by Dmitriy Khazanov, Tekhnika Molodyozhi Publishers, Moscow 1999.

In the months before Operation *Barbarossa*, German reconnaissance aircraft repeatedly flew over the USSR. Three were intercepted and shot down by MiG-3s of the 4th IAP/20th SmAD (*smeshannaya aviatsionnaya diveeziya*, Composite Air Division), flying out of a base near the Romanian border. As one of the first regiments to receive the MiG-3,

The crew of a Junkers Ju 88 bomber examines a destroyed MiG-3 at a captured Soviet airfield in 1941.

Fighter units of the Moscow PVO system equipped with the MiG-3

Unit	Location	Type of Aircraft	Number of Aircraft
16th IAP	Lyubertsy	MiG-3	42
		I-16	8
27th IAP	Klin	MiG-3	16
		I-16	31
	Kalinin	MiG-3	9
34th IAP	Vnukovo	MiG-3	27
		I-16	30
233rd IAP	Tushino	MiG-3	18
		LaGG-3	10
		I-16	18
1st OAE*	Khodynka	MiG-3	9
2nd OAE*	Ramenskoe (Zhukovskiy)	MiG-3	6
		I-16	4
		I-153	2

*Otdel'naya aviaeskadril'ya (Independent air squadron).

Damaged MiG-3 '2 Red' sits at a captured airfield, with Luftwaffe aircraft (a Dornier Do 17 and a Junkers Ju 52/3m g4e) in the background.

These destroyed MiG-3s photographed around November 1941 sport unusually high tactical numbers ('220 White' and '564 White').

Above: The Red Army Air Force lost a substantial number of its aircraft in the first hours and days of the Great Patriotic War. Many of them did not even manage to take off and were knocked out by Luftwaffe bombing raids, as nobody expected the treacherous aggression and the aircraft were not dispersed.

In addition to enemy action, the Red Army Air Force's MiG losses were caused by accident attrition, such as this radio-equipped example which looks like a write-off, although the pilot apparently walked away.

Above and below: These MiG-3s were captured intact by the advancing Wehrmacht in the first days of the war. The lower photo shows the state of the Red Army Air Force at the start of the war: a modern MiG-3 shares the airfield with obsolescent Polikarpov I-16 fighters and an even older Polikarpov R-5 recce biplane.

Above: They thought it was fun then... German soldiers pose beside a captured MiG-3 with not a care in the world. They would have different ideas soon enough!
Below: The MiG-3 in the foreground exhibits some fire damage, probably after being strafed by German fighters.

Above: The skin panels on this MiG-3 were probably ripped away by the blast wave of a bomb exploding nearby, exposing the fuselage structure.
Below: This MiG-3 was apparently damaged in a landing accident a few days before the invasion and abandoned in the midst of repairs when the Germans came.

Above: The men and officers of the Wehrmacht could not resist showing off like this with the 'vanquished' enemy. The hulk on the right is an Il'yushin IL-2.
Below: Another one bites the dust. Judging by the tall grass, this fighter had been sitting like this for a long time when the photograph was taken.

Above: Captain S. N. Polyakov, a 7th IAP pilot, sits on quick-reaction alert in his MiG-3 on the Leningrad Front in the summer of 1941. The fighter wears dark green/dark earth camouflage (one of the standard Soviet schemes of the period). There is no star insignia on the vertical tail. Note the radio aerial mast.

Another 7th IAP MiG-3 ('42 White', c/n 2267) about to taxi out on a sortie in October 1941. Again the aircraft wears dark green/dark earth camouflage; note the difference in insignia size and placement and the scuffed paint on the wing root. This example is not equipped with a radio and hence has no aerial mast.

Above: A MiG-3 about to take off from a dusty tactical airfield in the summer of 1942.

its pilots had been trained by test pilots sent to smooth the difficult conversion from biplane to monoplane – and a particularly tricky one to fly at that.

When German forces invaded the USSR in the early hours of 22nd June 1941, 37% of the aircraft equipping front-line fighter regiments were MiG-1s or MiG-3s; most of the others were Polikarpov biplanes or I-16s. The new Yak-1 and LaGG-1 were not yet in service in any appreciable number. MiG fighters served exclusively in 13 regiments and partially in a further six, which had not fully converted to them. Around the western border of the Soviet Union 917 MiG-1 and MiG-3 fighters were distributed, many of them in PVO units, but an additional 64 had been sent to naval units of the Baltic and Black Sea Fleets. Soviet military doctrine at that time decreed the launching of huge counter-attacks against any aggressor, and both ground forces and aircraft were deployed close to the frontier in attack formation. This was suicidal when trying to stop a Blitzkrieg, no lessons having been learnt from the successful German invasion of France and the Low Countries in the previous year. In addition, the forces were under strict orders not to provoke the German army and the aircraft were mostly arrayed in lines on the airfields.

Below: This MiG-3 is emblazoned *Smert' nemetskin okkupantam!* (Death to the German invaders!). Note the large star insignia thinly outlined in white.

Above: A MiG-3 with the tail number '6 Yellow' on a tactical airfield near Leningrad in 1942. One of the type's idiosyncrasies was poor visibility from the cockpit when on the ground because of the long nose and the cockpit itself being positioned well aft.

This 7th IAP MiG-3 ('27 Yellow'), caught by the camera at the moment of rotation, wears a non-standard streaked camouflage, probably applied in the field. Note that the sliding cockpit hood has been removed altogether – both to improve cockpit visibility and to facilitate baling out, should the need arise.

Above: Ground crews push back a MiG-3 at an airfield hidden in the midst of woodland.

This MiG-3 is armed with six RS-82 rockets on 3ROB-82 triple launchers. The stencil on the nose is not the aircraft's construction number as sometimes alleged; it reads *Redooktsiya 0,902*, indicating that this aircraft was powered by an AM-35 a with a reduction gear ratio of 0.902 (later aircraft had a ratio of 0.732).

Above: Lieutenant D. S. Titarenko, a 19th IAP/Leningrad PVO pilot, reports a 'kill' to Brigade Commissar F. F. Vetrov beside his MiG-3 on 6th July 1941. The Junkers Ju 88 destroyed by Titarenko was the first Luftwaffe aircraft shot down over Leningrad; the crew baled out and was captured.

A typical wartime publicity shot. Fighter pilots read letters from home between dogfights; life does not stop because there is a war on, after all. No, that's not battle damage to the tail of MiG-3 '54 White' but canvas covers piled on top of the stabiliser. Note that the cockpit hood is again deleted.

Above: A MiG-3 serialled '77 White' receives attention at one of the Soviet Air Force's aircraft repair shops; judging by the setting, this is not a mobile field maintenance shop (PARM) but a more permanent facility. Note the white-tipped spinner.

These MiG-3s wear late-style Soviet Air Force insignia heavily outlined in white for high visibility against the camouflage background in an attempt to avoid 'friendly fire' incidents. The unit number and the location are unknown.

Above: Alarm!!! Hot scramble! Flight leader Vasilevskiy fires a signal flare, ordering Lieutenant I. F. Goloobin to take off and intercept a German aircraft approaching Moscow. Goloobin became Hero of the Soviet Union on 4th March 1942 and scored 12 victories before being killed in action in October 1943.

The flight and ground crews of a Moscow Air Defence Force fighter unit kneel on one knee to take the Guards oath as their unit is awarded the elite Guards status in March 1942 for gallantry in combat, becoming the 12th GvIAP.

Above: MiG-3 '6 Yellow' takes off on another mission in defence of Leningrad in the summer of 1942. Note the underwing hardpoints.

This MiG-3 with the tail number '1 Blue' made a crash landing near Utti, Finland, in July 1942 after being damaged in an engagement with enemy aircraft. Note the ammunition belts which have burst out of their boxes.

Above: A flight of PVO MiG-3s patrols the skies of Moscow; the cockpits are open. Interestingly, the fighters are armed with RS-82s fitted with time-delay fuses for use against enemy aircraft.

Three factory-fresh winter-camouflaged MiG-3s await delivery at *zavod* No.1 in February 1942. No.2 in the line is inscribed *Za Stalina* (For Stalin), a common slogan in those days, while the farthest aircraft bears the legend *Za partiyu bol'shevikov* (For the Bol'shevik party).

In spite of being warned by his own spies and Winston Churchill, Stalin did not believe that Hitler would order an invasion. This folly had tragic consequences. Many airfields not only suffered onslaughts from the air but were also subjected to artillery bombardments. By sundown on the first day, 1,200 Soviet aircraft had been destroyed; this total included many of the MiG fighters from the five Defence Districts closest to the border: the Leningrad DD with eight Air Divisions, the Baltic DD with five, the Western DD with eleven, the Kiev Special DD with ten and the Odessa DD with four. Of these, the Western DD suffered most, losing 738 aircraft, of which 387 were fighters. The Odessa DD, although the smallest, had the greatest success; not only were the aircraft more prudently deployed but it had fighters on defensive patrols and it was also fortunate in that out of 827 fighters on its inventory over 100 were MiG-3s. On the first day it claimed to have destroyed 40 German aircraft for the loss of only 23 fighters.

Some senior officers, in spite of repeatedly reporting the German build-up and unsuccessfully requesting permission to take action, finally paid the ultimate price for the lack of foresight on the part of their superiors. Their only answer had been to avoid any action that could provoke a German attack. For example, Major General S. Chernookh, Commander of the 9th SmAD who had been awarded the title of Hero of the Soviet Union for his bravery in the Spanish Civil War, was executed as an 'enemy of the people' for losing 347 out of a total of 409 operational aircraft in his command on the first day.

Bad luck also contributed to the total losses. General Pavel F. Zhigarev, C-in-C VVS, had arranged the delivery 99 MiG-3s on the morning of 22nd June but all of them were destroyed. Fortunately a further 200 sent on 25th June successfully evaded this fate.

The shortage of pilots with the experience and confidence to fly the new monoplane fighter in battle gave rise to some anomalous situations. Many regiments had more aircraft than pilots qualified to fly them in combat. For example, in the 129th IAP at Tarnovo, very close to the Polish border, there were only 40 pilots qualified but 57 MiG-3s and 52 I-153 biplanes to be flown. The pilots were given the choice of the type to fly – and almost all selected the biplane.

A solution to this problem presented itself in a strange way. Alarmed at the success of the Luftwaffe and knowing the shortage of skilled pilots, the famous test pilot Stepan P. Sooproon wanted to demonstrate to other pilots that, adequately trained, they could fly the MiG-3 successfully in battle. It was also his suggestion that five regiments staffed by test pilots be formed from GK NII VVS, OKBs, factories and the VVS itself. Two were formed

Two 2nd GvIAP pilots – Z. A. Sorokin (left) and Sokolov – pose in front of a MiG-3. Note that the propeller spinner appears to be polished natural metal.

with MiG-3s: the 401st IAP commanded by Sooproon himself and the 402nd IAP commanded by Pyotr M. Stefanovskiy. As early as 2nd July 1941 the 401st IAP based at Zoobovo near Smolensk went into action; obviously Sooproon had not wasted much time with 'red tape', and in the first two days the regiment shot down eight enemy aircraft. On the third day, Sooproon shot down four invaders before he was killed in action. His outstanding bravery earned him a second HSU award – alas, posthumously. As soon as a cadre of experienced fighter pilots had been accumulated the surviving test pilots returned to their usual jobs.

The 402nd IAP went to the Leningrad sector, although the MiG-3 had not yet been passed for night flying; neither had the airfield been prepared for it. Shrugging off these difficulties, Captain Proshakov shot down a German bomber at night before landing with only his aircraft's landing lights to guide him.

Records state that at the beginning of the war, 22nd June 1941, the VVS had 407 MiG-3 fighters in service with its first-line regiments; on 1st January 1942 this number had increased to 686 but by 1st January 1943 had dwindled to 575. These figures exclude PVO and naval aircraft. As MiG-3 production had

Above: A MiG-3 pilot pores over a book while sitting in the cockpit of his fighter on quick-reaction alert (QRA) duty.

Above: The famous fighter ace Aleksandr I. Pokryshkin beside his MiG-3. By the end of the war he had shot down 59 German aircraft and become thrice HSU. He eventually rose to the rank of Air Marshal.

A MiG-3 captured by the Romanians and pressed into Romanian Air Force service.

ended in late December 1941, the only replacements for the 326 written off by the VVS in 1942 were the 30 built from components and those aircraft built in November and December 1941 and not delivered by the end of the year. In 1944 the VVS reported writing off 20 more MiG-3s, none of them to enemy action. Only one crashed, the rest were considered worn out; an indication that the type was not widely used by combat units.

Launchers installed on MiG-3s were originally intended to use RO-82 rockets against enemy aircraft but records of their use in this role are sparse. One story was told of an encounter involving a Major Babiy who was ordered to test these weapons. He took with him Lieutenant Semyonovich who was about to have his baptism of fire. Although ordered not to launch any rockets until instructed to do so, the inexperienced young pilot, when confronted by six Messerschmitt Bf 109s swooping onto them in a frontal attack, fired before the order was given. Four of the Messerschmitts exploded and the other two fled. On returning to base, Semyonovich was reprimanded for disobeying an order and for his pains was taken immediately on another sortie. Of course this success was not repeated very often, as the Germans soon developed countermeasures, but at least it made them think twice before mounting a frontal attack, a tactic that had been very successful with their latest cannon-armed fighters.

Very soon after the start of the war MiG-3s of the VVS, and sometimes those of the PVO, were being used to attack advancing German troops and in this role the rocket armament was more effective. Inevitably, carrying the launchers without rockets reduced top speed by about 15 km/h (10 mph) and manoeuvrability was also adversely affected. Hence on 10th May 1942 the GKO issued an order authorising removal of the rocket launchers at the commanding officers' discretion.

On 6th December 1941, as the Soviet Moscow counteroffensive opened, Stalin created a new elite, the Guards (Gvardiya). Regiments distinguishing themselves in battle were awarded the 'Guards' title (*Gvardeyskiy aviatsionnyy polk*, Guards air regiment) and six were created on that day. At a ceremony with all the staff from the unit kneeling, the proclamation from the GKO was read out and the commander received the new colours and title (the number was always changed) and all present repeated after him the Guards' oath '*to fight for your country and party to the last drop of blood and to conquer*'. Later this institution was extended to Divisions and Corps but the latter did not receive a new number. The 120th IAP of the 6th IAK PVO became the 12th GvIAP in March 1942, at a time when the regiment was equipped with MiG-3s.

Chapter 4

Experimental Versions

MiG-3 with leading-edge slats
In 1940 a standard MiG-3 was fitted with slats along the leading edges of the outer wing panels. The experiment was an expedient measure to test the effect of slats on the performance of a standard aircraft before fitting them to a MiG-3 modified to take an M-82A radial engine. It was a success and slats were subsequently installed, slightly shortened, on the I-210, the designation of the MiG-3 powered by an M-82A engine (see page 58).

MiG-3 reconnaissance version
An NKAP order of 3rd July 1941 instructed that four MiG-3s from the production series were to be fitted with AFA-I camera units specially developed at the OKO for these aircraft. On completion the aircraft were tested under service conditions; a fifth was then modified incorporating lessons learnt. After trials at GK NII VVS the modification was formally approved for VVS service.

MiG-3 with six-blade propeller
In September 1941 a single MiG-3 was fitted with an experimental six-blade propeller. The propeller had an increased diameter as compared to the standard VISh-61. Unfortunately no details of the test programme are known, nor is the aircraft type for which the propeller was intended.

MiG-3 lightened version
By way of an experiment in 1943 the NII VVS reduced the weights of two standard MiG-3s. One was reduced by the maximum possible amount, 187 kg (413 lb), to 3,098 kg (6,847 lb) in an attempt to increase the service ceiling. Tested at the NII VVS, an altitude of 11,750 m (38,500 ft) was achieved. No further details of the trials or of any subsequent action have been found.

MiG-3 with pressure cabin
(*izdeliye* KhS) (project)
One aim of the VVS was to investigate the possibility of fitting a pressure cabin to a MiG-3 to allow interception of German high-altitude bombers and reconnaissance aircraft. Aleksandr Ya. Shcherbakov had developed such a device at *zavod* No.482 in the Vladykino suburb of Moscow after experiments with three different designs of cabin on both the I-15 and I-153 biplane fighters. The final design was a welded duralumin cabin with 6-mm (0.23-in) thick Plexiglas windows and all apertures hermetically secured with rubber seals. These cabins were technically successful, but in practice they were found to be too heavy and the biplanes not powerful enough to carry the extra weight without an unacceptable degradation of performance. It was hoped that the MiG-3 would be powerful enough to handle the problem.

This picture taken on 18th September 1941 shows a MiG-3 equipped with an experimental six-blade propeller. Note the different colouring of the blades and the stripes on the black-painted ones.

Above and below: MiG-3 c/n 3595 was fitted experimentally with a 1,600-hp Mikulin AM-38 in 1941 in order to improve low-altitude performance. Note the restyled exhaust stubs and the the last two figures of the c/n on the tail.

Above: The MiG-9, aka MiG-3 M-82A, of 1941 was another attempt to improve low-altitude performance. This is the prototype (c/n 6502).
Below: The bulky Shvetsov M-82A radial engine changed the fighter's proportions completely.

Above and below: Front and rear views of the MiG-9 (MiG-3 M-82A). The single large oil cooler is located beneath the engine. Note the two large-diameter exhaust pipes.

A three-quarters rear view of the MiG-9. The aircraft was highly polished.

However, in 1941 the priority of zavod No.1 was to build up the output of standard fighters, which left no spare capacity for pressure cabin experiments. By the time production reached its peak, war had started and there was no course open to the plant but to defer the project until 1943 when NKAP ordered the I-222 (type 3A), described on page 58.

MiG-3 with sails (project)

Concern with the high landing speeds and corresponding long landing runs induced designer A.A.Sen'kov to promulgate a bizarre arrangement. Canvas horizontal sails attached to the sides of the fuselage of a MiG-3 would, he proposed, be retracted in flight but, during landing, would unfurl to create an extra wing and thus reduce landing speed. TsAGI's comment on this project was that the result was 'a very poor biplane and a corrupted monoplane'. Concern was also expressed that if such a landing were suddenly aborted the aircraft would not be able to go around again. Needless to say, few people other than the inventor took the idea seriously.

MiG-3 SPB variant (project)

This aircraft was proposed as a dive-bomber constituting part of a *Zveno* (Flight, as a tactical unit) 'mother ship/parasite aircraft' system developed by V. A. Vakhmistrov, hence the acronym SPB (*skorosnoy pikeeruyushchiy bombardirovshchik* – fast dive-bomber). This was a continuation of a fascinating system actually used in battle by the VVS whereby a Tupolev TB-3, an obsolete four-engined heavy bomber, carried two I-16SPB dive bombers, one under each wing, to within range of the target, hopefully still out of sight of enemy fighters. At this point the smaller aircraft would be released to carry out the bombing attack before flying back to the nearest friendly base. Further developing the concept, two MiG-3s would be strengthened to carry a FAB-250 (550-lb) bomb under each wing, while the 'mother ship' would be a Petlyakov Pe-8 (TB-7) four-engined bomber. Preliminary work on the Pe-8 was carried out at *zavod* No.124 *imeni. G. K. Ordzhonikidze* in Kazan' but pressure of other work caused the project to be abandoned.

Estimated design details of this Zveno Combination were: take-off weight 33,000 kg (72,900 lb), maximum speed 420 km/h (260 mph), operating height 5,000 to 6,000 m (16,400 to 19,700 ft), range 1,450 km (900 miles), flight duration 4.5 to 5.0 hrs.

MiG-7 (*izdeliye* 72 or MiG-3 with AM-37 engine)

It had been the intention to install a Mikulin AM-37 engine rated at 1,400 hp (1,030 kW) at 5,000 m (16,400 ft) in the *Samolyot* Kh (later I-200 and MiG-1), but the engine's protracted development forced the aircraft designers to replace it with the less powerful Mikulin AM-35A. In April 1941 the AM-37 passed its State acceptance trials and was intended to be mass-produced. In anticipation, an engine had been made available for trials and I-200 c/n 02, the second prototype MiG-1, was fitted with an example; these trials were unsuccessful and culminated in an engine-induced crash on 7th May 1941.

On 26th April NKAP ordered trials at *zavod* No.1 of a MiG-3 with the AM-37, appointing N. P. Baulin as test pilot and V. N. Sorokin as test engineer. Records show that on 13th May 1941 NKAP also asked the OKO to arrange comparative tests between MiG-3 aircraft fitted with Mikulin AM-37 and Shvetsov M-82A engines. Subsequently an AM-37 was installed in a production MiG-3 without any problems, the new engine being of similar dimensions to the standard AM-35A and also having identical attachment points. Flight test results were unsatisfactory, owing to the fact that not only was there a problem with the longitudinal stability of the aircraft but also the powerplant itself performed badly. It was decided that radical alterations to the aircraft were needed and that it would be wiser to cancel tests on the MiG-7 (*izdeliye* 72), as the

The MiG-9's engine cowling with the cowling panels closed (above) and open (below). Note the twin carburettor intakes and the adjustable forward-mounted cooling airflow adjustment flaps.

Above; One of the three pre-production MiG-9s deployed to the 260th Composite Air Division/7th Air Army on the Karelian Front.
Below: The pre-production MiG-9s differed from the prototype in having a Hucks starter dog on the propeller spinner.

aircraft was to be called, and the engine used instead on the DIS-200 twin-engined escort fighter. The engineless airframe was sent to a repair plant in the Moscow area for conversion to a standard MiG-3.

By this time the Germans had invaded and series production of the AM-37 was cancelled, as Mikulin's manufacturing resources had been entirely devoted to manufacturing the AM-38 which powered the Il'yushin IL-2 attack aircraft.

MiG-3 with an AM-38 engine

Many air battles on the Eastern Front were being waged below 4,000 m (13,100 ft) – a height at which, when compared with its opponents, the MiG-3 was at a distinct disadvantage. In an attempt to improve the MiG-3's performance at lower levels, one aircraft was re-engined with an AM-38 and fitted with an AV-5L-110A propeller. The AM-38 engine of the Il'yushin IL-2 was fully developed, in series production and rated at 1,600 hp (1,178 kW) for take-off and 1,550 hp (1,141 kW) at 2,000 m (6,560ft), making it an obvious choice. Since previous and current engines were of similar dimensions and weight, few alterations were required.

A production MiG-3 (c/n 3595) was accordingly refurbished and transferred to the Flight Research Institute (LII – *Lyotno-issledovatel'skiy instit*oot) where test pilot Yu. K. Stankevich made the first flight on 31st July 1941. A flight test programme followed immediately involving, in addition, GK NII VVS pilots A. G. Kochetkov, A. G. Kubushkin and A. M. Popel'nooshenko and LII test pilots Gheorgiy M .Shiyanov and A. V. Yumashev. Two series of trials were planned: the first with the aircraft as received and the second as further refitted by the OKB. Alterations made included redesigned exhaust pipes, bomb attachments and the system diverting exhaust gases into the fuel tanks. The standard machine had a top speed of 582 km/h (361 mph) at 3,400 m (11,200 ft) and the modified aircraft 592 km/h (367 mph) at the same altitude. Performance figures for the remodelled aeroplane can be found in the table on page 32 (see 'Basic Specifications of the I-200 (MiG-1) and MiG-3'). It is worth noting that the maximum speed at sea level had increased by 52 km/h (32 mph) with the new engine compared with the MiG-3's on State acceptance trials.

Below 4,000 m (13,100 ft) the MiG-3 with the AM-38 engine could successfully tackle all known enemy fighters and, with the time to turn through 360° reduced to 21 seconds, the aircraft would become a formidable opponent. Series production of the variant was recommended on the proviso that the tendency for the engine to overheat in ambient temperatures above 16°C (61°F) was eliminated.

On completing the tests at LII, MiG-3 c/n 3595 returned to *zavod* No.1 where the engine was replaced with another AM-38 and any other defects were rectified before sending it on to the NII VVS for State acceptance trials. After about 22 flights the aircraft returned to *zavod* No.1 on 28th September 1941 for modifications, including replacement of a deformed fuel tank and measures to improve the flying characteristics.

Tests resumed on 4th October but the following day, whilst determining the rate of climb and top speed at various heights, the fighter went into a dive and crashed, killing test pilot N .P. Baoolin. Eyewitnesses reported seeing two aircraft and hearing gunfire. Scrutiny of the wreckage showed that bullets had been fired from both ShKAS and BS machine-guns, indicating there must have been an air battle. Further investigation revealed the immediate cause of the crash to be damage to the tail unit that propelled the aircraft into an irrecoverable spin.

Although the State acceptance trials recommended series production of this variant, regrettably for the OKB, the scheme was dropped as all AM-38 engines had been allocated for IL-2 manufacture.

Ironically, later in the war when AM-35 engines were no longer available, about 80 MiG-3 airframes were made airworthy at VVS repair workshops by fitting refurbished AM-38s. Many of these aircraft were also given two 20-mm ShVAK cannon, each with 100 rounds of ammunition, for use by PVO regiments. Two aircraft of the VVS's 402nd IAP were re-engined with AM-38s in November 1941 and one (c/n 4184) was flown by the regimental commander Major K. A. Groozdev when he shot down two bombers.

MiG-9 (I-210, MiG-3 M-82A, *Samolyot* IKh or *izdeliye* 65)

On 13th May 1941 NKAP instructed the OKO to try out a MiG-3 with a Shvetsov M-82A two-row radial engine. The new variant was given the designation I-210 but was also known as MiG-9, MiG-3 M-82, Samolyot IKh or *izdeliye* 65. This modification was not so much an attempt to remedy the poor low-altitude performance but rather a direct result of the SNK order of 9th May 1941 to NKAP that the Mikoyan, Polikarpov, Lavochkin, Sukhoi and Yakovlev design bureaux utilise the M-82 on their aircraft. *Zavod* No.19 *imeni Stalina* in Perm' was then mass-producing the M-82 and, if used as a replacement engine for the MiG-3, the M-82 would allow more production capacity at *zavod* No.24 *imeni M. V. Frunze* to be given to the AM-38, the IL-2's engine. The M-82A was a 14-cylinder two-row air-cooled engine rated at 1,700 hp (1,251 kW) for take-off; at 6,500 m (21,300 ft) the power was reduced to 1,330 hp (979 kW).

I. G. Lazarev was given the task of installing the M-82A with as few alterations as possible to the front fuselage structure and the much more difficult task of designing an engine cowling that minimised drag. The opportunity was also taken to reinforce the armament compared with the standard MiG-3 and this comprised three 12.7-mm UBS machine-guns (200 rpg), firing through the propeller, and two synchronised 7.62-mm ShKAS machine-guns 650 rpg). In order to improve visibility an enlarged and extended cockpit canopy was fitted. To compensate for the lighter and shorter engine, stability was maintained by moving the wings back 10 cm (4 in). Leading-edge slats were introduced on the outer wings in an attempt to improve manoeuvrability and the tail fin was enlarged for better longitudinal stability.

After installation of the M-82A engine the first experimental prototype (c/n 6501) made its maiden flight on 23rd July 1941, piloted by M. I. Martselyuk, and shortly after was transferred to LII for its factory flight tests. A second prototype (c/n 6502) was used for weapons trials from 25th August 1941 with A. P. Yakimov as pilot. At this stage only the three UBS machine-guns had been fitted. Three pre-production aircraft (c/ns 6503 to 6505) were completed by the end of the year.

It had been estimated that the I-210 would have a maximum speed of 630 km/h (391 mph) at 6,500 m (21,300 ft), 530 km/h (329 mph) at sea level and be able to climb to 5,000 m (16,400 ft) in 4.9 minutes. The results obtained in the course of State Acceptance Tests (which were completed by the end of August) were very disappointing, with a top speed of only 540 km/h (335 mph) at 5,000 m (16,400 ft). Some blame was levelled at the poor carburettor operation and unsuitable AV-5L-156 propeller, which had been fitted instead of an AV-5-127A. In addition to this, there had been a significant increase in drag caused not only by the enlarged fuselage cross-section area but, more particularly, by the poor design and inadequate sealing of the engine cowling.

Undeterred by these poor performance figures and impressed by the armament and perceived potential of the design, the military asked for an acceleration of the improvement programme.

On 11th September 1941 NKAP, keen to help resolve the problems, instructed S. N. Shishkin, head of TsAGI, to formulate recommendations by the 15th of the same month for the most effective propeller. What was more, he also had to collect relevant flight data on fighters and bombers powered by the M-82 engine so that by 25th September the best design of engine cowling for the MiG-9 could be determined. By 20th October it had become necessary to extend this investigation at TsAGI to include also Yak and LaGG aircraft being fitted with this engine.

In September a MiG-9 was subjected to wind tunnel tests at TsAGI which revealed the full magnitude of the problem with the engine cowling. However, in October 1941, with the enemy nearing the gates of Moscow, both *zavod* No.1 and its OKO were evacuated to Kuibyshev together with the MiG-9s. It was not until January 1942 that aircraft No.6502, suitably modified with a new cowling, was flown again during manufacturer's tests, piloted by V. N. Savkin. At the same time its spin characteristics were determined and turned out to be very similar to those of the production MiG-3.

On 16th March 1942 an NKO decree reorganised the OKO as an independent OKB with a new site of its own, complete with experimental factory, in Moscow. It is possible, but unlikely in the absence of further evidence, that the OKO had become an OKB in Kuibyshev before this date. The team was no longer a department in a factory to which they owed allegiance but the downside was that, by the same token, the factory was no longer under any obligation to give their designs priority for mass production. OKO *zavoda* No.1, now designated OKB *zavoda* No.155 (often shortened to OKB-155), expended a great deal of effort in rebuilding and extending the derelict site they had been given. By April all the team had returned from evacuation in Kuibyshev and moved into their 'new' premises. Encouraged by the news that a new aircraft factory known as *zavod* 30 (named 'Znamya Truda', 'Banner of Labour', in 1963) had been opened on the evacuated site of *zavod* No.1, the new OKB proceeded to modify all five MiG-9s.

In early June 1942, three MiG-9s (c/ns 6503 to 6505) were sent to the 34th IAP/6th PVO Fighter Corps on the Kalinin Front for operational trials to receive their baptism of fire. They were armed with three synchronised 12.7-mm UBS and two additional synchronised 7.62-mm ShKAS machine-guns. After serving with the 34th IAP until 27th October 1942 the three aircraft were returned to the OKB for further work on their power units.

Meanwhile, aircraft No.6502 was sent to the Flight Inspection section of the VVS and later to the 12th GvIAP of the 6th PVO Corps. State acceptance trials were conducted by engineer I. G. Glazarev and pilot V. Ye. Golofastov from 7th September 1942, by which time the fighter's armament had been reduced to three 12.7-mm BS machine-guns. Repeated return visits to the OKB for modifications to the engine and propeller prolonged the duration of the tests to two months and ended unsatisfactorily; the flying characteristics of the MiG-9 proving inferior to those of the La-5 and Yak-7. Manoeuvrability was not as good as that of the MiG-3 and heavy vibrations were felt in the tail unit.

In spite of failing the State acceptance trials three MiG-9s (c/ns 6501, 6502 and 6503), after further modification at the OKB, were transferred to the 260th SmAD/7 VA (*vozdooshnaya armiya*, Air Army) where they served on the Karelian Front. VVS records show that three MiG-9s were withdrawn from service in 1944.

Performance figures determined in the State acceptance trials are shown in the table on page 62, together with those of the standard MiG-3 and I-211 for comparison. They show that, compared with the MiG-3, top speed at sea level had fallen from 495 km/h (307 mph) to 475 km/h (295 mph), time to 5,000 m (16,400 ft) had risen from 6.5 to 6.7 minutes, and service ceiling had fallen from 11,500 m (37,700 ft) to 8,700 m (28,500 ft).

MiG-9Ye (I-211, *Samolyot* Ye)

Undeterred by the disappointing performance of I-210, the OKB decided in the last quarter of 1942 that more radical changes were required. A MiG-9 was tested at TsAGI in their large T-1 wind tunnel and the data collected was used to redesign the aircraft. To improve the likelihood of success a more advanced engine was used; Shvetsov could now offer the M-82F radial engine which delivered 1,850 hp (1,362 kW) for take-off with the same maximum power, 1,330 hp (979 kW), at the lower altitude of 5,400 m (17,700 ft). The aerodynamic shape of the fuselage front end was given a larger cross-section, mating more smoothly with the redesigned cowling. To reduce drag the adjustable flaps of the exhaust outlets were rearranged on the sides of the fuselage, the oil cooler inlets repositioned in the leading edges of the wing roots, and the oil cooler buried inside the airframe. An even larger tail fin was fitted and the cockpit moved 24.5 cm (9⅝ in) back. Armament was also improved by installing two synchronised 20-mm ShVAK cannon, one each side of the lower part of the engine cowling.

This MiG-3 was preserved in the hangar of TsAGI's Bureau of New Equipment (BNT) in the late 1940s. Unfortunately it did not survive; all that is left now for posterity is a rather crude mock-up constructed in the 1960s.

Above and below: The MiG-9Ye (alias I-211 or *samolyot* Ye) represented an attempt to improve the disappointing performance of the MiG-9 (MiG-3 M-82). The revised shape of the cowling and the twin exhaust stubs are well visible, as are the redesigned main gear doors.

Above and below: Two more views of the MiG-9Ye. Note that the oil cooler is housed internally to reduce drag. The upper photo shows the bulletproof glass panel aft of the pilot's seat.

Unfortunately all this took time and the assembly of the I-211 did not begin until December 1942 and was completed on 28th January 1943. Factory tests started on 12th February, allowing test pilot V. N. Savkin to make the maiden flight on 24th February 1943. The performance of the new fighter was excellent and much better than that of the 1942 versions of the Yakovlev Yak-9 and Lavochkin La-5. Below is a table showing the performance figures of the I-211 compared with the MiG-3 and the I-210 (MiG-3 M-82A). One particularly striking parameter concerns the take-off weight, which had been reduced by 312 kg (690 lb) from 3,382 kg (7,474 lb) for the I-210 to 3,070 kg (6,785 lb) for the I-211. Some commentators suggest this weight reduction resulted from the change to an all-metal structure but confirmation of this has not yet been found. This, coupled with the reduction in drag, gave the I-211 a sparkling performance with a maximum speed of 670 km/h at 7,100 m (23,300 ft) and a time to 5,000 m (16,400 ft) of only 4.0 minutes.

Originally the OKB had planned to build a total of 10 MiG-9Ye fighters for the VVS in the first quarter of 1943, but factory trials were not completed until the first quarter of 1944. By this time jet fighters were appearing in Britain and Germany and work on the MiG-9Ye ceased with only a single prototype built. Had the MiG-9Ye been offered at an earlier date, it would have stood a better chance of achieving series production. We can only surmise that this could have been achieved if the OKB had restricted the number of new designs.

It is ironic that Polikarpov, whom Mikoyan replaced as chief designer at *zavod* No.1, suffered a similar fate earlier in 1943 when his I-185 was rejected for series production in favour of keeping current fighters on the production lines while improving their design. The GKO (*Gosoodarstvennyy komitet oborony*, State Committee for Defence) had made that most difficult of wartime decisions: whether to continue with existing designs or to start mass production of a new type with the inevitable decrease in the number of aircraft manufactured. History supports the wisdom of their decision.

MiG-9 with M-90 engine (project)
While preparations for the first flight of the MiG-9Ye were taking place in February 1943 the OKB staff were studying how to fit the Shvetsov M-90 engine into the MiG-9 airframe. This new 18-cylinder radial was expected to develop 2,000 hp (1,472 kW); however, the project failed to proceed because no engine was made available.

MiG-9 with AM-39 engine
The Russian State Archive of Economics (RGAE – *Rosseeyskiy gosoodarstvennyy arkhiv ekonomiki*) f.8044, op.1, d.1026 contains a report on the implementation of NKAP Order No.523ss of 31st August 1943 concerning the production of high-altitude fighters. This contains an order to Polikovskiy, chief of TsIAM (*Tsentrahl'nyy naoochno-issledovatel'skiy institoot aviatsionnovo motorostroyeniya*, Central Aero Engine Research Institute). He was detailed to produce a report by 15th October 1943 on the results of 25 hours' ground testing of a Mikulin AM-39 engine destined for a MiG-9. No evidence has been found of a MiG-9 being flown with such an engine. The only MiG aircraft known to have flown with this power plant at about this time was the I-220.

While it is difficult to see any logic behind changing the engine of a MiG-3 from an in-line model to radial and then back again to an in-line configuration, the report was an official NKAP document. It is unlikely that the reference to the MiG-9 is an error and therefore we must conclude that the designation MiG-9 had wider application than is generally believed.

MiG-9 with an AM-39 engine with a TK-2B turbosupercharger
RGAE f.8044, op.1, d.1026 also refers to a government report that *zavod* No.300, which housed the Mikulin OKB, had supplied TsIAM with an incomplete motor of this type on 5th September 1943 when the need to redesign the frame on which the engine would be mounted became evident. The file also shows that an AM-39 engine was tested from 8th September but that the tests were stopped on 27th September because of a leak in the water radiator and the radiator was returned to *zavod* No.300 for repairs. The 25-hour tests were to be completed by 15th October.

A second AM-39 engine earmarked for actual installation in an aircraft at *zavod* No.155 started ground tests at *zavod* No.300 on 20th September, but these were stopped on 22nd September because bronze particles had been found in the oil filter. Delivery of this motor to *zavod* No.155 was delayed until 2nd October. The aircraft was prepared for this motor to be fitted but further work was delayed for lack of an engine. Whilst this was going on, *zavod* No.35 delivered on schedule a four-blade propeller to *zavod* No.155 on 15th September. Meanwhile, instructions were given to TsIAM to deliver a TK-2B turbo-supercharger to *zavod* No.155 on 10th September; it was sent on 11th September.

In spite of this burst of activity in September and October 1943, there have been no subsequent reports so far discovered of a MiG-9 flying powered by an AM-39 with a TK-2B turbosupercharger. However in 1943, OKB-155 built the I-221 (type 2A) with that powerplant. For reasons outlined in the section on the 'MiG-9 with an AM-39 engine', we must again conclude that the designation MiG-9 had wider application than is generally believed.

MiG-9 with Pratt & Whitney R-2800-63 engine with S-23 turbosupercharger (project)
In March 1944 the OKB were considering the installation of a 2,250-hp (1,656-kW) Pratt & Whitney R-2800-63 radial engine with a General Electric S-23 turbosupercharger into a MiG-9Ye airframe. A maximum speed of 740 km/h (459 mph) at 10,000 m (32,800 ft) and a service ceiling of 14,500 m (47,600 ft) with a take-off weight of 3,800 kg (8,400 lb) were predicted. After a presentation of the concept to the NKAP on 8th April 1944, no further design work was done. The MiG-9 designation was later reused for Mikoyan's first jet fighter which flew in 1946.

Comparative performance data for the MiG-3 and MiG-9

	MiG-3	MiG-3 M-82A (I-210)	MiG-9Ye (I-211)
Engine	AM-35A	M-82A	M-82F
Rated output at take-off, hp (kW)	1,350 (993)	1,700 (1,251)	1,850 (1,362)
Span	10.2 m (33 ft 6 in)	10.2 m (33 ft 6 in)	10.2 m (33 ft 6 in)
Length	8.25 m (27 ft 1 in)	8.1 m (26 ft 7 in)	8.0 m (26 ft 3 in)
Wing area, m² (sq.ft)	17.44 (188)	17.44 (188)	17.44 (188)
Empty weight, kg (lb)	2,699 (5,965)	2,762 (6,104)	2,590 (5,724)
Take-off weight, kg (lb)	3,355 (7,415)	3,382 (7,474)	3,070 (6,785)
Wing loading, kg/m² (lb/sq.ft)	192 (39.4)	194 (39.8)	176 (36.1)
Top speed at sea level, km/h (mph)	495 (307)	475 (295)	n.a.
Top speed, km/h (mph)	640 (397)	565 (350)	670 (415)
at altitude, m (ft)	7,800 (25,600)	6,150 (20,200)	7,100 (23,300)
Climb to 5,000m (16,400 ft), minutes	6.5	6.7	4.0
Service ceiling, m (ft)	11,500 (37,700)	8,700 (28,500)	11,300 (37,100)
Range, km (miles)	820 (509)	1,070 (663)	940 (583)
Take-off run, m (ft)	347 (1,138)	410 (1,345)	n.a.
Landing run, m (ft)	410 (1,345)	535 (1,755)	n.a.

Chapter 5

To Build a Better 'Three'

The I-230 Series

I-230 (MiG-3U, Type 'D' or MiG-3D)

After series production of the MiG-3 at *zavod* No.1 in Kuibyshev had stopped on 23rd December 1941, the OKO redoubled their efforts to design a successor. In addition to fitting radial engines to the MiG-3 airframe the designers decided to hedge their bets by continuing to develop a variant with an in-line engine. It was obviously advantageous to try to use as many as possible of the production tools and jigs that had been employed in the manufacture of the MiG-3, and this idea strongly influenced the design.

On 16th March 1942, now elevated to the status of OKB with its own experimental factory, the design team commenced moving to their new site in Khodynka, then a north-western suburb of Moscow. Converting the stretch of wasteland with a few primitive buildings euphemistically called *zavod* No.155 into a true design bureau took time and energy and it was May 1943 before the first prototype, designated I-230 by NKAP and known to the OKB as *izdeliye* D, was built.

By this time an NKAP instruction of 27th February 1943 had asked for an interceptor for the PVO with a gross weight of 3,100 kg (6,850 lb), top speed of 670 km/h (415 mph), a service ceiling of 12,500 m (41,000 ft) and the ability to climb to 10,000 m (32,800 ft) in 13 minutes. The lack of a suitable engine was again the main problem. As no other Mikulin in-line engine was available, all AM-38F production being reserved for the IL-2, the OKB were driven to installing a reconditioned AM-35A with 0.732 reduction gear. There was no chance of this engine being returned to series production, but it did allow the new I-230 fighter to be developed whilst Mikulin perfected his next engine.

While superficially resembling the MiG-3, the I-230 had the latter's large ventral radiator located beneath the cockpit replaced by an OP-310 type glycol radiator buried further inside the fuselage so that a shallower air duct could be used. Grouped with the duct were the inlets for the type 533 oil cooler; the air from this and the OP-310 exited through flaps in the underside of the wing centre section. In the leading edges of the wing roots were the inlets feeding the superchargers. In addition, there was a system for diluting the oil with petrol to ease start-ups in very cold weather but this was not tested in the trials. Individual exhaust stubs replaced the previous twin arrangement. The propeller was an AV-5L-126A with a diameter of 3.2 m (10 ft 6 in). All in all, the engine installation was very elegant.

The fuselage of the I-230 was slightly longer (37 cm or 14½ in) than that of the MiG-3 to contain the new larger (440-litre/97-Imp.gal.) single fuel tank behind the engine which replaced the four separate tanks of its predecessor. However, the two centreplane tanks of the MiG-3 could be re-installed and used in overload conditions. Behind the wider cockpit the fuselage was cut back to allow a backward extension of the transparency, giving a better rear view. Because the cockpit was repositioned slightly further aft the field of forward vision was more restricted when landing and taxying. An upward-opening door immediately aft of the cockpit allowed access to the radio, compressed-air and oxygen bottles.

Fin area was increased and the rudder extended forward between the two upper hinges, giving an aerodynamic balance. The horizontal tail was moved back and set 20 cm (8 in) higher to be nearly level with the top of the fuselage. On the first prototype the radio mast in front of the cockpit is not shown in all photographs.

To reduce the amount of scarce metal used the welded tube truss in the tail section and the centre section of the fuselage aft of the engine firewall was replaced by a single monocoque structure of three veneer plies, each 1 mm thick. This eliminated the duralumin side panels of the MiG-3 but the tail fin itself was made of duralumin and easily removable. The main wing spar and centre section structure were still of 30KhGSA steel but in the centre section, where the main spar passed through the water radiator tunnel, its web was replaced by a truss structure. The outer wing structure no longer relied on *del'-ta-drevesina* and wood but was constructed of T-shaped pieces of chrome-manganese alloy and duralumin walls. Leading-edge slats were installed and the aileron balance enhanced. Because of the slats the pitot tube was fixed below the starboard wing. On the redesigned and strengthened main undercarriage, better shock absorbers were used and the wheel well closure on retraction now consisted of a flap on the wheel and a separate rectangular door.

A PBP-1A gunsight was installed for the two 20-mm synchronised ShVAK cannon mounted on top of the engine, each with 150 rounds. No provision was made for fitting underwing racks to carry bombs, rockets or additional guns. An RSI-3 radio transmitter and RSI-4 receiver were fitted and the oxygen equipment contained a KPA-3*bis* with a 4-litre (0.88-Imp. gal.) supply vessel.

Having their own factory, the OKB were able to impart a superb finish to the skin, which added to the beauty of airframe. Test pilot S. V. Savkin made the maiden flight of the first prototype (c/n D-01) on 31st May 1943. Factory tests were successfully completed towards the end of July with 28 flights totalling 13 hours 26 minutes, in spite of problems encountered with the oil system. State acceptance trials were conducted at GK NII VVS by engineer A. S. Pozanov and test pilot V. I. Khomyakov from 28th July to 6th August 1943 during which 23 flights, including ten at high altitude, were made totalling 15 hours 26 minutes. A maximum speed of 505 km/h (313 mph) at sea level was recorded, increasing to 656 km/h (407 mph) at 7,000 m (23,000 ft); service ceiling was 11,900 m (39,000 ft), time to 5,000 m (16,400 ft) was 6.2 minutes.

With a second-hand obsolete engine the performance parameters almost reached the NKAP requirements of 27th February 1943, and were creditable enough for the OKB to develop the type into the I-231. Pilots liked the comfortable cockpit and well-arranged instruments; many flying characteristics were good but the fighter was very difficult to land. However, they considered it should not go into service until its faults, particularly the tail unit vibrations and defective oil system seals, were corrected. So bad were the oil leaks that on landing the I-230 was seen to have its fuselage covered with oil, especially if it had been operating above the engine's maximum power-rated altitude. Further information on the I-230 is contained in the table at the end of the I-231 section on page 69.

Five more aircraft were built at *zavod* No.155 in July and August with construction numbers D-02 to D-06. Again, all had reconditioned engines but to improve high-altitude performance D-04 received larger wings with a span of 11.14 m (36 ft 0½ in) instead of the 10.2 m (33 ft 5½ in) span of all the other

Above and below: The first prototype of the I-230 (aka MiG-3U), c/n D-01. These views illustrate well the fighter's elegant lines. Note the individual exhaust stubs, the 'solid' wheel disks, the shallow glycol radiator bath and the enlarged engine air inlets in the wing roots.

Above and below: The same aircraft at GK NII VVS during State acceptance trials. Note the addition of a radio aerial mast. The design of the main gear doors is similar to that of the I-211 (MiG-9Ye)

Above and below: Front and rear views of the first prototype MiG-3U (I-230) during State acceptance trials. No insignia was carried on the wing upper surfaces.

Above and below: The I-230 was plagued by oil leaks during flight tests, especially in high-altitude flights. Here is the outcome of one of the test flights: the port side of the fuselage and the port wing root are liberally covered in oil.

Above and below: The second prototype MiG-3U (c/n D-02) was appropriately serialled '02 White'. Note that the radiator bath is deeper, with an undivided air intake, and the engine air inlets in the wing roots are also enlarged.

Another view of the second prototype MiG-3U (I-230).

MiG-3 variants; the longer wings had an area of 18.22 m² (196 sq.ft).

On completion of the State acceptance trials all six I-210s were flown by Lt. P. A. Zhuravlyov and examined by mechanics of the 12th GvIAP/6th IAK, PVO. As a result, D-01, D-03, D-04 and D-06 joined the regiment on the Kalinin Front in August 1943 but D-02 and D-05 remained at *zavod* No.155 to await replacement engines. During this period D-02 was also fitted with longer wings of the same type as those on D-04 and, after the installation of the engine on 10th October 1943, joined the 177th IAP, but D-05 was sent to *zavod* No.34 for further repairs. Because of the problems encountered, the PVO subsequently decided not to accept any more I-230s. Furthermore, the type was never going to be series-produced as it was not considered worthwhile to restart production of the AM-35A. By September 1943 a new in-line liquid-cooled engine, the AM-39A, was ready for testing.

In PVO service the I-230 was known as the MiG-3U (*ooloochshennyy*, improved); some sources also suggest that MiG-3D (*dahl'niy*, long-range) was the designation but a possible reason for this is that the 'D' in *izdeliye* 'D' was mistakenly assumed to be the suffix of MiG-3 rather than the OKB name for this design.

I-231 (Type '2D', MiG-3DD or MiG-3U with AM-39)

In September 1943 the new inline engine, the Mikulin AM-39A derived from the AM-35A via the ill-fated AM-37, was available for OKB-155 to use on the I-230 airframe. The engineer charged with the task of modifying the I-230 was V. N. Sorokin. Notable changes made to the I-230 c/n D-01 included lowering the horizontal tail by 20 cm (8 in) to revert to the original MiG-3 position in an effort to eliminate the vibrations of the tail structure that had plagued the I-230. The fuel load was increased slightly from 324 kg (716 lb) to 333 kg (736 lb) and the ammunition supply from 150 to 160 rounds per gun. To maintain the engine at a reasonable temperature with the increased power of 1,800 hp (1,325 kW) for take-off a new radiator was designed, increasing the cooling surfaces from 2,480 to 3,000 cm². Incorporated in the radiator housing was the intercooler for the supercharger.

The first flight took place on 19th October 1943 with V. N. Savkin at the controls. Respon-

Table showing the data for the I-230 and I-231 and that of the MiG-3 for comparison:

	MiG-3	I-230 (D-01)	I-231
Engine	AM-35A	AM-35A	AM-39A
Rated output at take-off, hp (kW)	1,350 (993)	1,350 (993)	1,800 (1,325)
Span	10.2 m (33 ft 6 in)	10.2 m (33 ft 6 in)	10.2 m (33 ft 6 in)
Length	8.25 m (27 ft 1 in)	8.62 m (28 ft 3¼ in)	8.62 m (28 ft 3¼ in)
Wing area, m² (sq.ft)	17.44 (188)	17.44 (188)	17.44 (188)
Empty weight, kg (lb)	2,699 (5,965)	2,627 (5,806)	2,583 (5,708)
Take-off weight, kg (lb)	3,355 (7,415)	3,260 (7,205)	3,287 (7,264)
Wing loading, kg/m² (lb/sq.ft)	192 (39.3)	187 (38.3)	188 (38.6)
Top speed at sea level, km/h (mph)	495 (307)	505 (313)	n.a.
Top speed, km/h (mph)	640 (397)	656 (407)	707 (438)
at altitude, m (ft)	7,800 (25,600)	7,000 (23,000)	7,100 (23,300)
Climb to 5,000m (16,400 ft), minutes	6.5	6.2	4.5
Service ceiling, m (ft)	11,500 (37,700)	11,900 (39,000)	11,400 (37,400)

Above and below: 'White Tip shark'. The second prototype MiG-3U had white tips to the spinner and the vertical tail.

Above: An I-230 (MiG-3U), nearest the camera, during service trials with the 12th GvIAP/6th PVO Fighter Corps. The next aircraft in the line is a Yak-7PD, another experimental type.

sibility for the engine in the factory trials was given to I. V. Kotov, with A. V. Fufurin taking charge of the airframe. During a flight on 5th November the supercharger disintegrated but Savkin with great skill managed an emergency landing at Noginsk, for which he was awarded the order of the Red Star. Factory trials resumed on 23rd November after replacement of the engine; a top speed of 707 km/h (438 mph) at 7,100 m (23,300 ft), a time to 5,000 m (16,400 ft) of 4.5 minutes and a service ceiling of 11,400 m (37,400 ft) were recorded.

Before the aircraft was sent to GK NII VVS for its State acceptance trials on 26th February 1944, a new AV-5L-126Ye propeller was fitted which was 25.3 kg (60 lb) lighter. During the trials on 8th March 1944 the I-230 was wrecked in a landing accident with Pyotr M. Stefanovskiy at the controls. Apparently the flaps had not lowered for some reason, and when the wheel brakes also failed the aircraft ran off the runway and stood on its nose. It was sent back to the OKB for repairs, returning on 12th May. Shortly afterwards, on 19th May 1944, the trials stopped after the engine failed when the boost was used. All development of the I-231 was terminated when the decision was taken not to put the AM-39 into series production, as no other suitable engine was available.

Below: The prototype of the improved I-231 (2D) during manufacturer's flight tests. The lower-set horizontal tail is clearly visible.

Above and below: Two more views of the I-231. The fighter was prevented from entering production by the unavailability of its intended AM-39 engine.

Chapter 6
A New Line Emerges

The I-220 Series

I-220 (Type 'A', MiG-11)

Although the MiG-3 was a high-altitude fighter, the service ceiling of the production aircraft was only 11,500 m (37,700 ft), making it unable to intercept the Junkers Ju 86P photographic reconnaissance aircraft when it appeared over the USSR in 1941. Operating at altitudes of 13,000 m (42,600 ft) rendered the Ju 86P invulnerable. Most of the air operations on the Eastern Front took place below 6,000 m (19,700 ft) and by July 1941 a requirement for a high-altitude interceptor was deemed necessary. OKO *zavoda* No.1 were asked to design such an aircraft.

Interrupted by the need to evacuate to Kuibyshev, it was the end of the year before a project outline could be prepared. Powered by a Mikulin AM-37 engine, the projected I-220 was a larger aircraft than the MiG-3 with an estimated top speed of 680 km/h (422 mph) at 7,600 m (24,900 ft) and a time to 5,000 m (16,400 ft) of 5.3 minutes.

The armament was to consist of two wing-mounted 20-mm ShVAK cannon, each with 150 rounds, plus two synchronised 12.7-mm UBS machine-guns each provided with 200 rounds in the wing centre section; this arrangement was chosen to avoid dazzling the pilot when the guns were fired at night.

On 10th March 1942 approval was given by Lieutenant General I. F. Petrov, chief engineer of the VVS, for the project to be included in the experimental aircraft budget for 1942.

The I-220 was known within the OKB as type 'A' but would be designated MiG-11 if it entered mass-production. A new AM-39 engine was to be installed, since development of the AM-37 had ceased. On 27th June 1942 a mock-up was examined and provisionally accepted with formal approval from the mock-up review commission being given on 20th August.

Two prototypes were ordered but another dilemma arose because the AM-39 was not immediately available. As a temporary measure the first prototype was to be given an AM-38F, the standard engine for the Il'yushin IL-2 at the time. It developed 1,700 hp (1,250 kW) for take-off and 1,500 hp (1,100 hp) at 4,800 m (15,700 ft) and for the I-220 was given a 3.6-m (11.8-ft) diameter AV-5L-126A three-blade propeller and individual exhaust stacks for each cylinder.

To reduce drag the air intakes for the glycol radiators were placed in the wing centre section leading edges, with intakes for the superchargers and oil coolers in the wing roots. The box-type glycol radiators themselves, situated further back in the centre section behind the main spar, had controllable exit flaps about half-way along the wing upper surface. Relocating the air intakes entailed reducing the armament to two synchronised nose-mounted 20-mm ShVAK cannon with 150 rpg, but this was altered by the mock-up review commission to four under overload conditions. In fact only two cannon were actually installed in the first prototype.

A completely new wing design was used with a TsAGI laminar-flow airfoil having a maximum thickness at 40% chord. A horizontal centre section spanning 3.96 m (13.0 ft) was constructed mostly of D16 duralumin but with 30KhGSA steel booms on the main spar which continued through the mainly wooden outer panels. In plan view the outer wing panels had straight trailing edges but the leading edges were swept back. Full-length slats extended along the leading edge of the outer

An artist's impression of a preliminary development project version of the proposed MiG-11 fighter. Note the aft-retracting main gear units, the wheels rotating through 90° to lie flat in the wings; a feature that was not used on the actual aircraft in the I-220 series.

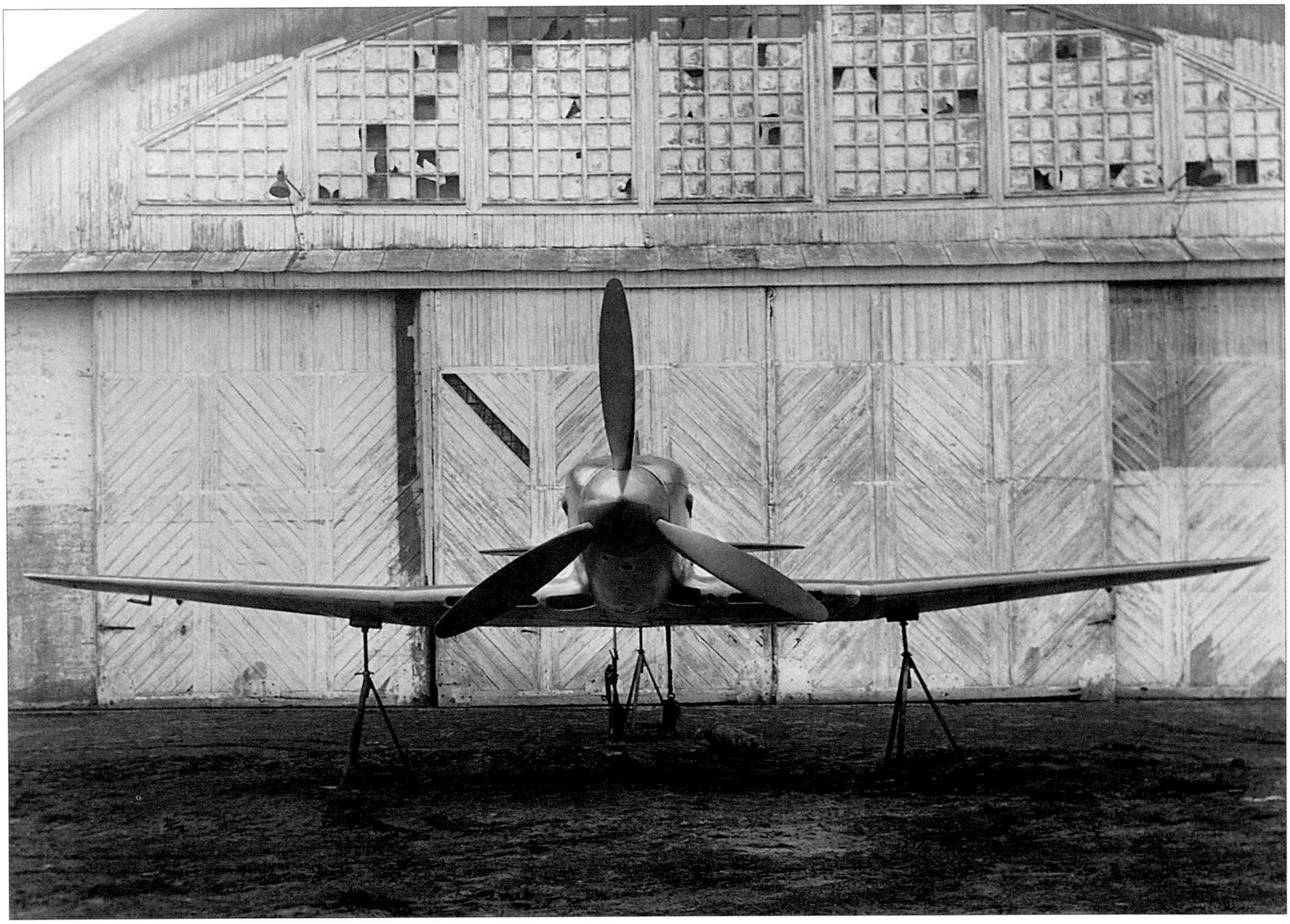

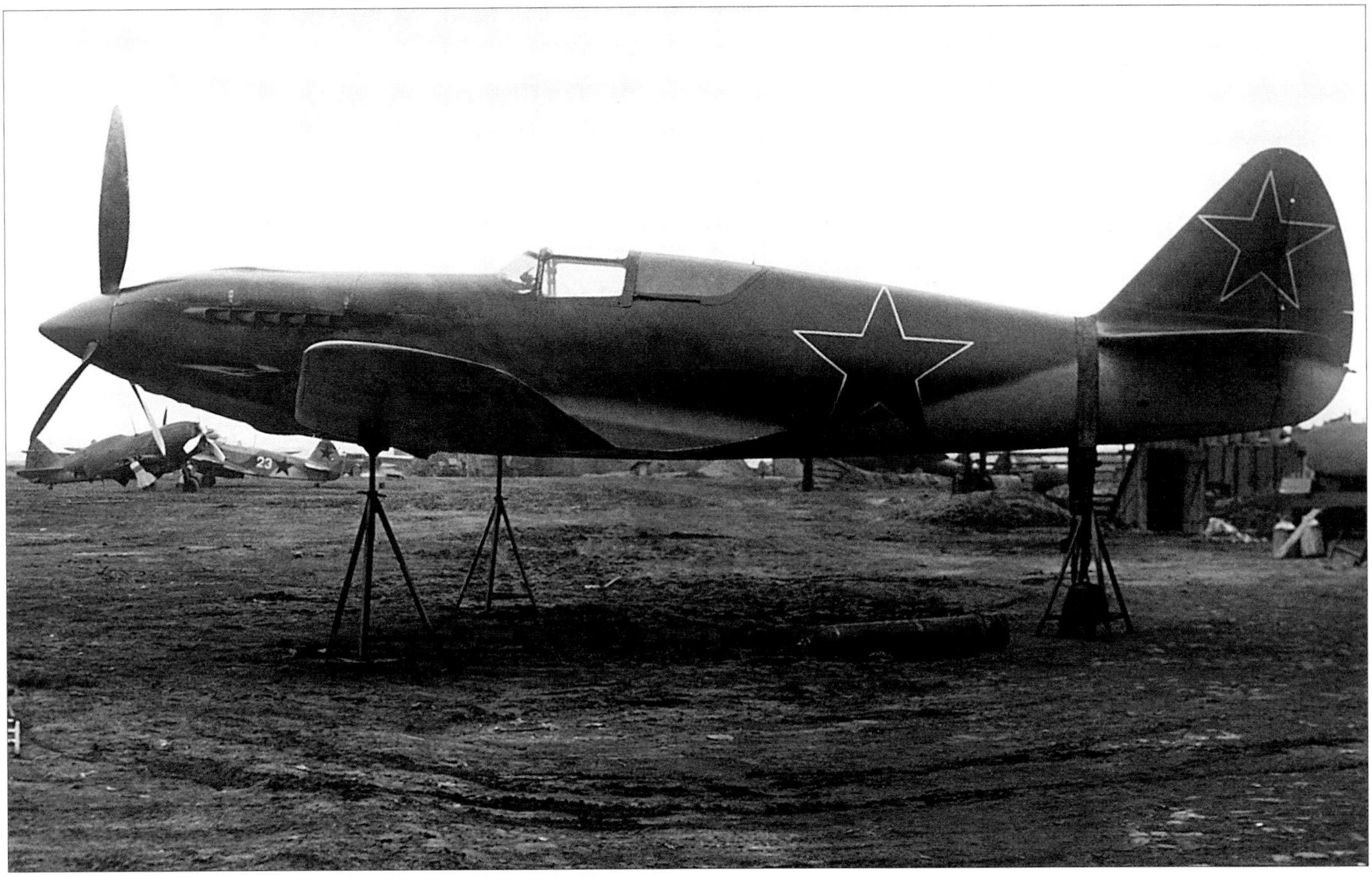
23

Opposite page, above and below: The first prototype I-220 (A) (c/n 01) was originally flown with an AM-38F engine pending delivery of the intended AM-39. It is seen here trestled for landing gear operation checks during manufacturer's tests. Note the MiG-9 (MiG-3 M-82) minus outer wings sitting under wraps in the background in the lower photo; the aircraft has been modified by fitting a new propeller featuring wide-chord blades with cropped tips!

This page, top: The first prototype I-220 (still powered by an AM-38F) at GK NII VVS during Stage A of the State acceptance trials.

Right and above right: The first prototype's AM-38F engine and engine bearer could be completely exposed. Note the two cannon positioned low on the sides of the engine crankcase, with their ammunition boxes just aft of the engine, and the oil tank above the engine's reduction gearbox.

Above and below: I-220 (A) c/n 01 as originally flown. Note the old-style star insignia and the different camouflage scheme. These views show well the large forward angle of the main landing gear struts and the inboard half-forks characteristic of the first prototype.

Two more views of the same aircraft, illustrating the engine cooling radiator air intakes (outboard) and the carburettor inlets (inboard) incorporated into the wing leading edge.

Above and below: I-220 (A) c/n 01 following re-engining with an AM-39 and repainting (note the new-style insignia heavily outlined in white). It is seen here during renewed manufacturer's flight tests.

A three-quarters rear view of the upgraded first prototype I-220.

wings and large split flaps were attached to both the centre section and outer wing; the ailerons were also split.

The fuselage structure was mainly *shpon* with a steel tube cradle for the engine and a duralumin tail unit bolted onto the main fuselage longerons. As with the MiG-3U (I-230), the horizontal tail was mounted closer to the top of the fuselage, with a longer span of 3.75 m (12 ft 3½ in). In contrast to the MiG-3 the cockpit was positioned further forward, giving improved forward vision and providing the pilot with a more comfortable ride, as he was closer to the centre of gravity.

The main undercarriage design was innovative, having a longer stroke of 515 mm (20.3 in) and a levered suspension. Retraction was pneumatic and the inward-retracting struts had wheels with 650 x 250 mm (25.5 x 9.84 in) tyres. The cable-operated aft-retracting tailwheel had a 350 x 125 mm (13.77 x 4.9 in) tyre.

Altogether six self-sealing fuel tanks of coated rubberised fabric were installed (four in the wings plus two larger ones in the fuselage resting on a duralumin cradle) and contained in fireproof varnished plywood boxes. A wide unpressurised cockpit was given a rearward-sliding canopy over a shelf for a radio located behind the seat.

In September 1942 the first prototype I-220 (c/n 01) emerged from *zavod* No.155 and, after ground tests, commenced its factory trials on 20th November with A. G. Broonov as chief project engineer and A. I. Zhookov as project test pilot. As the delivery of the AM-38F was delayed, an AM-38 engine was installed in its place and on 26th December the I-220 took to the air for the first time. After the flight the aircraft went straight into the workshops for work on the powerplant; problems were found with the supercharger and metal chips were discovered in the oil. However, an AM-38F had finally arrived and was installed on 8th January 1943, replacing the original engine. Furthermore, it was discovered that the wing centre section needed strengthening; flights were resumed on 7th February when this and other tasks were completed. Initially the new undercarriage retraction system would not operate properly but this problem was soon resolved.

Basic flight characteristics of the aeroplane were determined in mid-March and revealed that the I-220 had great potential. Even with the AM-38F it had a good top speed: 576 km/h (357 mph) at sea level and 624 km/h (387 mph) at 2,650 m (8,700 ft); and an excellent rate of climb, taking only 4.6 minutes to reach 5,000 m (16,400 ft).

When the first AM-39 (engine number 3900) arrived in April 1943 some modifications were required to the engine cooling system and to the air passages leading from the supercharger to the cylinders. The first flight with the new engine did not take place until 25th May 1943. In July the performance with the new engine was determined: with a top speed at sea level of 614 km/h (381 mph) increasing to 697 km/h (432 mph) at 7,800 m (25,600 ft), the I-220 was able to climb to 5,000 m (16,400 ft) in 4.5 minutes and 8,000 m (26,200 ft) in 8.2 minutes. The trials were interrupted on 21st August 1943 when Zhookov was forced to land the fighter on one wheel after the port main undercarriage failed to drop. Thanks to his skill the aircraft suffered minimum damage.

Problems arose with the new engine, necessitating five visits to the workshops, and on 27th September it became necessary to re-install a standard production AM-38F. Flight tests resumed on 1st October but on 2nd October I-220 c/n 01 was damaged again in another landing accident.

After more repairs it was subsequently decided to send the aircraft for its State acceptance trials with the AM-38F – later to be replaced by the AM-39 in the hope that it would have been improved by then. From 22nd October 1943 to 2nd January 1944 the aircraft was at GK NII VVS, where engineer A. S. Rozanov and test pilot Pyotr M. Stefanovskiy examined it. During these tests the

79

Above and below: The second prototype I-220 (A), likewise re-engined with an AM-39 and repainted. Note the different design of the main gear units with the half-forks on the outer side of the wheels, allowing the latter to be replaced without removing the gear doors.

Above and below: I-220 c/n 01 with an AM-39 engine at GK NII VVS during State acceptance trials. The shadow gives some indication of the outer wing sweep angle. Note the addition of the aerial mast.

Front and rear views of the AM-39 powered I-220 c/n 01 at GK NII VVS, showing the fairly wide landing gear track.

Another view of the re-engined first prototype I-220, showing the high-quality surface finish.

maximum speed with the AM-38F engine was 572 km/h (355 mph) at sea level and 622 km/h (386 mph) at 2,600 m (8,500 ft); at maximum boost these speeds were increased to 608 km/h (377 mph) and 652 km/h (404 mph) respectively. Pilots who flew the I-220 praised its flying characteristics and heavy armament and the final report stated that, even with the AM-38F engine, up to a height of 3,500 m (11,500 ft) it outperformed all the other experimental aeroplanes being tested. The authorities asked for the I-220 with the AM-39 engine to be brought for its State acceptance trials as soon as possible. However, two faults had been highlighted: buffeting of the tail unit and the tendency for a wing to drop at high angles of attack. On the fighter's return to the OKB on 8th February 1944, test pilot A. P. Yakimov started work on these problems. It transpired that tail buffeting was caused when the radiator flap was opened at certain speeds.

Work had started in 1943 on I-220 No.2 which was planned to be moved to the airfield on 4th December 1943. This was to be the pattern aircraft for series production with four synchronised 20-mm ShVAK cannon in the nose. The other major external difference between I-220s c/n 01 and c/n 02 was in the design of the undercarriage leg, which was altered to facilitate wheel changing. On the original design the wheels were outboard of the main forked leg but on No.2 they were moved to be inboard, thus enabling the wheel to be changed without removing the undercarriage doors. It had been the original intention to install an AM-38F engine (to be replaced later with an AM-39) but instead it was decided to start with the newer engine, as sufficient data on the AM-38F version could be obtained from the first prototype. No accurate details have been found on the date of the first flight of I-220 c/n 02 but it is thought to have taken place in early 1944. This supposition is borne out by records showing that it had been rebuilt as the first prototype of the I-225 by 9th May 1944; first flight in that guise was on 21st July.

I-220 No.1 went into the workshop on 8th March 1944 to receive a series-built AM-39 (No.45302) and on 10th May was ready to begin additional factory tests carried out by engineer A. G. Broonov and test pilot A. P. Yakimov and completed on 28th June. This time 695 km/h (431 mph) was reached at 7,500 m (24,600 ft). Two more cannon were added and ammunition was reduced to 100 rounds for each of the four guns.

On 14th July I-220 No.1 with the AM-39 engine started its State acceptance trials with engineer V. I. Alekseyenko and project test pilot D. G. Pikoolenko. During the trials the engine had to be replaced yet again by another AM-39 (No.45306) and flights resumed on 15th September. A top speed of 668 km/h (414 mph) at 6,800 m (22,300 ft) was noted, as were a time to 5,000 m (16,400 ft) of 6.3 minutes and a service ceiling of 11,000 m. (36,100 ft). Before trials had been completed, all testing ceased at the request of Artyom I. Mikoyan and the I-220 returned to the OKB where the decision had been made to redesign the aircraft. It had become clear that in spite of building an aeroplane with a good performance and heavy armament, it would never be able to fulfil its design objective of reaching 13,000 m (42,600 ft) without a more powerful engine. As a consequence, I-220 c/n 02, which had completed fewer flying hours than c/n 01, was rebuilt as the I-225.

More data on the I-220 is shown together with that of other 'A' series fighters in the table after the section on the I-225 (page 93).

I-221 (Type '2A')

Encouraged by the ability of a Yak-9 powered by a Klimov M-105PD engine to reach 12,000 m (38,400 ft), NKAP asked OKB-155 on 14th June 1943 to produce by 1st September a high-altitude fighter capable of operating up to 14,000 m (46,000 ft). The success of the Yak-9 was due to the exhaust-driven turbo-superchargers fitted to the engines and the OKB were instructed to use the same type on

83

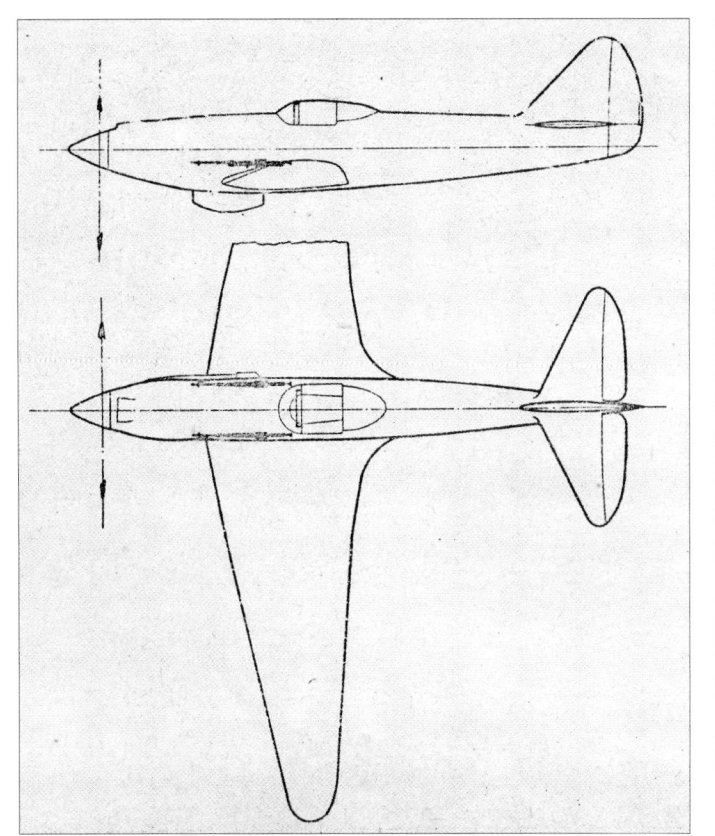

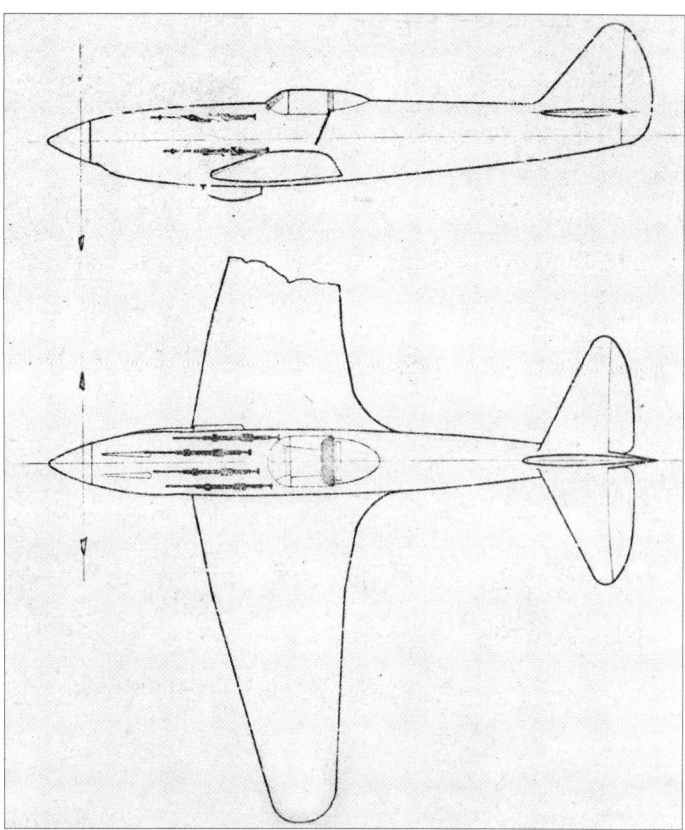

Above: These drawings from the project documents show the I-224 (left) and the I-225 (right); note the cannon placement.
Below: One of the I-220 series fighters in one of TsAGI's wind tunnels. Note the airflow visualisation tufts.

a suitable development of the I-220 to be called I-221 or type '2A'. As usual, engine development was running late and the aircraft was not completed until 28th October 1943.

Delivering 1,750 hp (1,288 kW) for take-off, the AM-39A was modified in readiness for the two TK-2B turbosuperchargers that would enable the engine to maintain its maximum rated power up to 13,000 (42,600 ft). The reduction gear ratio was changed from 0.732 to 0.59 and a four-blade AV-9 propeller 3.5 m (11 ft 5¾ in) in diameter installed. Wing span was extended to 13.0 m (42 ft 7¾ in), increasing the wing area to 22.38 m² (241 sq.ft). The armament comprised two 20-mm synchronised ShVAK cannon, each with 100 rounds, installed low down in the nose. Estimated performance gave a top speed of 685 km/h (425 mph) at 12,500 m (41,000 ft) and a service ceiling of 15,000 m (49,200 ft). The fighter was expected to be able to fly for 20 minutes at 14,000 m (46,000 ft).

After the cannon were test fired the I-221 was moved to the airfield on 5th November 1943. The intention was to hold the first flight on 22nd November with pilot P. A. Zhooravlyov, seconded from the 12th GvIAP, at the controls but engine problems delayed it until 2nd December. Eight flights totalling 3 hours had been conducted and a top speed of 690 km/h (428 mph) reported by the OKB when, on the 7th February 1944 at 9,000 m (29,500 ft), the pilot baled out and the aircraft was destroyed. The commission investigating the crash concluded that the pilot mistook flames from the TK-2B turbosupercharger exhaust plus smoke in the cockpit for an engine fire.

No photographs of the I-221 have survived but the OKB published a three-view drawing.

I-222 (Type '3A')

NKAP asked OKB-155 to continue developing a high-altitude fighter based on, and designed with the same performance parameters as, the I-221 but with the addition of a pressure cabin. Designated I-222 (type '3A') the prototype was to be ready by 15th March 1944.

Although still under development, an AM-39B engine with two TK-2B turbosuperchargers (some sources say one TK-300 but this is unlikely) was selected. It produced 1,750 hp (1,288 kW) for take-off and 1,430 hp (1,052 kW) at 13,200 m (43,300 ft); the actual engine received was the first prototype AM-38B. At first it drove an AV-5L three-blade propeller, later replaced by the four-blade AV-9L-230 optimised for high-altitude flight. The cockpit was pressurised and constructed of AMTs alloy with the aft-sliding canopy sealed by inflatable tubes. Air-conditioning was fitted and behind the canopy the fuselage was cut away to improve rearward vision. A large ventral inlet was located under and jutting slightly in front of the wing centre section to supply air into a heat exchanger feeding the pressure cabin. Engine and oil cooling radiators were both positioned in the wing roots. The engine air supply system included an air-to-air heat exchanger that replaced an air-to-water unit; the weight this change saved helped to compensate for the extra weight of the pressure cabin. Flexible fuel tanks were located in the fuselage and the wing centre section, the latter having the oil tank in its leading edge. Both tailplane and tail fin were slightly larger than the equivalent on the I-221.

Estimated top speed was 689 km/h (427 mph) at 12,500 m (41,000 ft), with a service ceiling of 14,000 m (46,000 ft). Two synchronised 20-mm SSh-20 nose-mounted cannon were installed with 100 rpg. A bulletproof windscreen was added and armour installed behind the pilot's head.

The prototype was rolled out at *zavod* No.155 on 28th April 1944 and took to the air for the first time on 7th May; the pilot was probably A. P. Yakimov, although A. I. Zhookov has also been suggested. An NKAP document dated 1st June referred to K. P. Kovalevskiy as chief engineer with A. P. Yakimov as test pilot for the factory tests. Between 26th July and 9th August the I-222 was tested in the large wind-tunnel at TsAGI, resulting in a new design of wing slats and an enlarged intercooler. Factory tests restarted on 1st September with Igor' I. Shelest as test pilot, but he crashed in another aircraft on 3rd September and was replaced by G. M. Shiyanov. Altogether 39 flights were completed in the tests, during which the maximum height reached was 12,000 m (39,400 ft), but it was established that the AM-39B with two TK-2B turbosuperchargers should be limited to 11,300 m (37,100ft). Above that height oil and fuel pressure fell and engine running became irregular.

From 19th October 1944 the I-222 was transferred to LII for further tests, as instructed by NKAP. After three flights a decision was taken on 26th January 1945 to send the engine to *zavod* No.300 for further development work. It was duly returned and in July it was refitted to the airframe, but a loss of oil pressure was noted at 6,000 m (19,700 ft) and after a total of five flights the engine was again returned to *zavod* No.300 where it stayed in spite of pressure from NKAP in the form of an order to return the engine by 10th August 1945. With no engine, all development work on the I-222 ceased.

The sole I-222 (3A) powered by an AM-39B with two TsIAM TK-2B turbosuperchargers. The aircraft appears to be unpainted.

Above and below: Two more views of the I-222 as originally flown with an AV-5L series three-blade propeller. These photos illustrate the turbosupercharger housings aft of the exhaust stacks, the lowered rear fuselage decking to improve rearward view and the large ventral water radiator bath.

Above and below: The I-222 following painting and a refit with an AV-9L-230 four-blade propeller. It is seen here during manufacturer's flight tests. Note the air intake above the propeller spinner.

Above and below: two more views of the I-222 in ultimate configuration. The aircraft was painted green with pale blue undersurfaces and red propeller blade tips.

Above and below: While basically similar in appearance to the I-222, the I-224 differed in having a more blunt spinner, wider-chord propeller blades and a single TK-300B turbosupercharger on the starboard side. Note the large metal sheet protecting the skin which extends almost all the way to the tail.

Above: This view of the I-224 (4A) illustrates the rounded ventral intercooler housing and the restyled engine inlet/oil cooler air intakes in the wing roots.
Below: The prominent water radiator air outlets on the inner wing upper surface were another recognition feature of the I-224.

OKB data recorded a top speed of 691 km/h (428 mph) at 12,500 m (41,000 ft), a time to 5,000 m (16,400 ft) of 6 minutes and a service ceiling of 14,500 m (47,600 ft). Some of these figures are possibly extrapolated, as there is no other record of an altitude greater than 12,000 m (39,400 ft) being reached.

I-224 (Type '4A')

Yet another high-altitude fighter prototype was built by OKB-155 after *zavod* No.300 had developed a new exhaust-driven turbosupercharger designated TK-300B. The unit was fitted onto the right-hand side of an AM-39FB (c/n 2) and a huge 3.5-m (11.5-ft) diameter four-blade AV-9L-26B propeller was used, the blades having a maximum chord of 400 mm (15.7 in). One commentator suggests that the original powerplant was an AM-39B with an AMTK-1 turbosupercharger and that later the more powerful AM-39FB replaced the former. Once again the basic design of the airframe was that of the I-221 and I-222 but the heat exchanger intake was larger, and the coolant radiators were moved back to the leading edge of the wing centre section with two distinctive outlets on both upper wing surfaces. A welded duralumin sheet provided the structure for the pressure cabin, which received air from the supercharger compressor. Armament was one 20-mm synchronised Berezin B-20 cannon with 100 rounds and provision for a second in overload configuration, but some sources suggest two 20-mm ShVAK cannon were actually installed.

Rolled out on 4th August 1944, the I-224 first flew on 16th September; factory trials followed immediately with K. P. Kovalevskiy as chief engineer and G. M. Shiyanov as test pilot (other sources have the first flight on 20th October 1944 with A. P. Yakimov as pilot). Only five flights had been completed when the aircraft crashed when forced-landing on 28th September after engine failure. After repairs, on 23rd December it went to LII for further tests. In February 1945 metal chips were discovered in the oil filter, necessitating an engine change. Later, in July, the TK-300B turbosupercharger was replaced after vibrations were reported, but the aircraft had not yet flown higher than 13,700 m (45,000 ft). However, the I-224 reached its service ceiling of 14,100 m (46,250 ft) before completing these trials on 26th October 1945; one source suggests 14,200 m (46,600 ft) was achieved. Maximum speed at sea level was 574 km/h (356 mph) and it was estimated to be able to reach 693 km/h (430 mph) at 13,100 m (43,000 ft).

After refurbishment at the OKB the I-224 was ready for its State acceptance trials at GK NII VVS but *zavod* No.300 requested changes be made to the air duct between the intercooler and carburettors in an effort to overcome the surge problem affecting the the TK-300B. A variable flap was fitted to allow excess air to spill out into the atmosphere when surging occurred. Shortly after, *zavod* No.300 decided to replace the AM-39FB with the AM-44 which had direct fuel injection instead of carburettors. The replacement engine arrived on 31st July 1946 but had so many development problems that the I-224 was never submitted for State acceptance trials. On 30th November 1946 all work on the I-224 was stopped by ministerial decree.

I-225 (Type '5A')

While the first prototype I-220 was performing its factory tests, A. I. Mikoyan had decided that there was no likelihood of a conventional Soviet aeroengine powering one of his fighters to 14,000 m (45,900 ft). Therefore he rebuilt the second prototype with a new engine, the AM-42B fitted with a TK-300B turbosupercharger on the right-hand side and driving a 3.6-m (11.8-ft) diameter three-blade AV-5LV-22A propeller. The engine was rated at 2,000 hp (1,470 kW) for take-off and 1,750 hp (1,288 kW) at 7,500 m (24,600 ft). Note that the I-224 with the TK-300B had not yet flown. A. G. Broonov was entrusted with this project and the designation I-225 (type '5A' within the factory) was given to this new high-altitude fighter prototype. The aircraft had a ventral heat exchanger air intake and a pressurised air-conditioned cockpit. Armament was four synchronised, nose-mounted 20-mm Shpital'nyy SSh-20 cannon but it was intended to replace them later with series-produced Berezin B-20s of similar calibre. To protect the pilot's back, 9-mm (0.35-in) armour was installed and both windscreen and canopy rear section were formed from 64-mm (2.5-in) bulletproof glass.

On 9th May 1944 I-225 c/n 01 was completed by the factory and its first flight took place on 21st July, probably with A. P. Yakimov at the controls. Factory trials began immediately and at normal rating a top speed of 580 km/h (360 mph) at sea level was recorded, rising to 721 km/h (447 mph) at 8,850 m (29,000 ft); the climb time was 4.5 minutes to 5,000 m (16,400 ft) and 7.9 minutes to 8,000 m (26,200 ft). No performance figures for maximum military power are available because, unfortunately, on 9th August, the aircraft experienced engine failure at low altitude during its fifteenth flight, caught fire and was destroyed in the subsequent crash. Yakimov, the pilot, survived with burns.

A second prototype I-225 (c/n 02) was completed on the 20th February 1945, but instead of the planned AM-43 an AM-42FNB (some archival sources quote AM-42FB) was installed with a new AMTK-1A turbosupercharger and an AV-5L-22B propeller. Again the armament was four SSh-20 cannon subject to replacement on later aircraft by the Berezin B-20 which had just entered series production. First flight took place on 14th March 1945, piloted by A. P. Deyev, with factory trials following immediately. On 26th April, after the sixteenth flight, the second I-225 crashed as it was taking off from a small airfield near the village of Loozgarino when the port undercarriage prematurely retracted; the aircraft veered into a ploughed field and groundlooped, breaking off its rear fuselage and tail unit.

Refitted with a new rear fuselage, the second prototype continued its factory trials in June 1945 and registered a top speed of 560 km/h (347 mph) at sea level and 726 km/h (450 mph) at 10,000 m (32,800 ft), with a time of 4.0 minutes to 5,000 m (16,400 ft) and 8.6 minutes to reach 10,000 m (32,800 ft).

State acceptance trials began at GK NII VVS on 30th October 1945; originally it had been 25th October, but surging in the

The I-225 (5A) c/n 02 powered by an AM-42FB (c/n 01) with an AMTK-1A turbosupercharger.

Above and below: Seen here during manufacturer's flight tests, the second prototype I-225 featured a TK-300B turbosupercharger on the starboard side, with a black 'anti-soot' panel painted on aft of it. Note the extreme aft location of the star insignia on the fuselage.

TK-300B turbosupercharger was experienced during a check-out flight and the tests were delayed. On 10th November the casing of the turbosupercharger burnt out and was replaced in December, but on the second test flight in January 1946 more problems surfaced. This time the TK-300B was removed, the diffuser replaced and a new inlet duct fitted between the intercooler and carburettors. As on the I-224, the duct was fitted with a controllable flap to spill excess air when surging started.

During the third test flight on 27th January 1946 severe engine vibrations were experienced at 6,000 m (19,700 ft); zavod No.300 recommended changing to the new AM-44 engine which had fuel injection instead of carburettors. Tests were interrupted while the aircraft went back to zavod No.155 on 13th February 1946 for the engine to be changed. Unfortunately the new engine did not arrive there until 6th April and it was not until 31st May 1946 that I-225 c/n 02 flew again. At the request of zavod No.300 tests were once more delayed until the TK-300B was replaced by a new turbosupercharger designated AMTK-1A. The new engine combination was eventually ground tested in June 1946 but a significant number of defects were found and I-225 c/n 02 never went for State acceptance trials. All work on the I-225 was finally terminated on 11th March 1947; piston-engined fighters were now an anachronism.

I-240 project

In the article *Aleksandr Mikulin, a Legendary Man* by Lev Berne and Vladimir Perov published in *Dvigatel'* (Engine) magazine Nos. 2 and 3-2001, a reference confirms that, in April 1944, a request was made by the VVS to the OKB of Mikoyan and Guryevich for a single-seat high-altitude fighter powered by an AM-43 fitted with a turbosupercharger. Performance requirements were a service ceiling of 12,000 m (39,400 ft) and a top speed of 700 km/h (434 mph) at 8,000 m (26,200 ft). The OKB is said to have developed the I-240 design with that powerplant and the maximum speed was expected to be between 700 and 750 km/h (434-465 mph), but with a revised armament of one 45-mm and two 20-mm cannon. No record of this aircraft being built has been found. The I-240 project would seem to have been superseded by the I-250.

One possible explanation as to how this designation arose is that perhaps it was to have been given to I-225 c/n 02. This was intended to have an AM-43 with TK-300B turbosupercharger but, as so often happened, the AM-43 was unavailable when the second I-225 was completed in February 1945. An AM-42NFB was substituted and so the I-240 designation was not required. Its armament of four 20-mm cannon, top speed of 726 km/h (450 mph) at 10,000 m (32,800 ft) and service ceiling of 12,600 m (41,300 ft) were close to the VVS requirements.

Details and performance data of 'A' series high-altitude interceptors:

Designation	I-220	I-220	I-221	I-222	I-224	I-225
Type	A	A	2A	3A	4A	5A
Source of data	State Tests	State Tests	OKB	OKB	Factory Tests	Factory Tests
Engine	AM-38F	AM-39	AM-39A + 2 x TK-2B	AM-39B + 2 x TK-2B	AM-39FB + TK-300B	AM-42B + TK-300B
Rated output at take-off, hp (kW)	1,700 (1,250)	1,800 (1,325)	1,750 (1,288)	1,750 (1,288)	1,750 (1,288)	2,000 (1,472)
Span	11.0 m (36 ft 1 in)	11.0 m (36 ft 1 in)	13.0 m (42 ft 7¾ in)	13.0 m (42 ft 7¾ in)	13.0 m (42 ft 7¾ in)	11.0 m (36 ft 1 in)
Length	9.5 m (31 ft 2 in)	9.5 m (31 ft 2 in)	9.5 m (31 ft 2 in)	9.6 m (31 ft 6 in)	9.6 m (31 ft 6 in)	9.5 m (31 ft 2 in)
Wing area, m² (sq.ft)	20.38 (219.4)	20.38 (219.4)	22.38 (241)	22.38 (241)	22.38 (241)	20.38 (219.4)
Empty weight, kg (lb)	2,936 (6,488)	3,103 (6,858)	n.a.	3,167 (6,999)	3,105 (6,862)	3,010 (6,652)
Take-off weight, kg (lb)	3,574 (7,899)	3,835 (8,475)	3,800 (8,398)	3,790 (8,376)	3,780 (8,354)	3,900 (8,619)
Wing loading, kg/m² (lb/sq.ft)	175.4 (29.6)	188.2 (38.6)	169.8 (34.8)	169.3 (34.8)	168.9 (34.7)	191.4 (39.3)
Top speed at sea level, km/h (mph)	608 (377)	625 (431)	n.a.	n.a. (356)	574 (347)	560
Top speed, km/h (mph)	652 (404)	695 (431)	690 (428)	691 (428)	693 (430)*	726 (450)
at altitude, m (ft)	2,600 (8,500)	7,500 (24,600)	n.a.	12,500 (41,000)	13,100 (43,000)	10,000 (32,800)
Climb time to 5,000 m (16,400 ft), minutes	4.6	4.5	n.a.	6.0	4.8	4.0
Service ceiling, m (ft)	n.a.	11,000 (36,100)		14,500 (47,600) †	14,100 (46,200)	12,600 (41,300)
Landing speed, km/h (mph)	130 (81)			127 (79)	134 (83)	

* Estimated
† Questionable

Three views of I-225 c/n 01 powered by AM-42B c/n 02 with a TK-300B turbosupercharger on the starboard side. The aircraft was converted from I-220 c/n 02, hence the high rear fuselage decking.

Chapter 7

The 'Half-Jet'

Mikoyan's First Step Towards Jet Propulsion

I-250 (Type 'N', MiG-13)

By January 1944 information had reached the USSR of the existence of successful British and US jet aircraft and of the rocket and jet aircraft about to come into service with the Luftwaffe. On 18th February 1944 the GKO recognised that research on jet propulsion, which had been under more than one Commissariat, should be gathered together under NKAP. As a result, NII-1 NKAP was formed on 28th February from GIRT (*Gosoodarstvennyy institoot reaktivnoy tekhniki*, State Institute of Jet Propulsion Technology) which previously had reported directly to the SNK. NKAP was to present to the GKO by 15th March specific proposals to remedy the situation. The outcome of this was an instruction from NKAP on 30th May to Lavochkin, Mikoyan, Sukhoi and Yakovlev to design and build reaction-propelled aircraft as a matter of the utmost urgency. By then Arkhip M. Lyul'ka had begun testing his VRD-2 turbojet but, after noting the experience of other OKBs with underdeveloped rocket and ramjet engines, OKB-155 looked for a more mature product. The Sukhoi and MiG design bureaux both selected the VRDK (*Voz**dooshno**-rea**kt**ivnyy **dvigatel' kompres**sornyy*), a motor compression engine that K. V. Kholshchevnikov had started to develop in 1942 at TsIAM.

In 1940 Vladimir M. Myasishchev had projected a high-speed bomber with ramjet accelerator units positioned inside the fuselage to avoid the reduction of top speed, rate of climb and manoeuvrability caused by the excessive drag of the large nacelles. This raised the question of the behavioural characteristics of ramjets in such a location and at TsAGI G. N. Abramovich, a section head, was given this problem to solve. Theoretical studies showed that the restricted airflow inside the fuselage was insufficient to produce the necessary thrust and the project was discontinued.

However, the lack of theories for reaction propulsion systems was recognised by Abramovich and he persuaded the authorities to set up a department at TsAGI for research into them. Abramovich concluded that using a conventional piston engine to drive a compressor, thereby increasing the airflow velocity, could solve the problem raised by Myasishchev. To enable him to proceed with studies of aircraft having *motor compressor engines*, as they were called, a TsAGI department was established in March 1942 directed by Abramovich to study all reaction power systems. This department included an aircraft design team and sections to focus on the working and combustion processes of these systems. Aviation fuel was used and a traditional piston engine drove the VRDK's compressor. The reaction engine then had a maximum total operating time of ten minutes, making it suitable as a booster on propeller-driven aircraft.

The main engine selected by both MiG and Sukhoi was a 1,650-hp (1,230-kW) Klimov VK-107R (M-107R; R = *redook*tornyy – geared) driving a VISh-105SV three-blade tractor propeller and also, through an auxiliary gearbox, the compressor of the VDRK, which boosted the total output at 7,000 m (23,000 ft) to 2,500 hp (2,061 kW). More than 95% of total power of the VK-107R was transmitted by the engine's reduction gear to the 3.1-m (10 ft 2-in) propeller to facilitate take-off. Once airborne, to attain maximum speed a clutch behind the crankshaft was engaged, driving a step-up gearbox (13:21 ratio) to a shaft which transferred power to a compressor situated in a large duct in the lower part of the fuselage. Air, part of which was bled off to the oil cooler, reached this duct from an inlet under the spinner and was also used to cool the main radiator located immediately behind the compressor. A secondary pipe in the top of the duct fed air to the main engine's supercharger. When power was transmitted to the compressor, airflow was vastly increased and greater pressure in the secondary upper pipe also boosted output from the piston engine. As the air flowed through the main duct it was mixed with petrol sprayed from seven nozzles

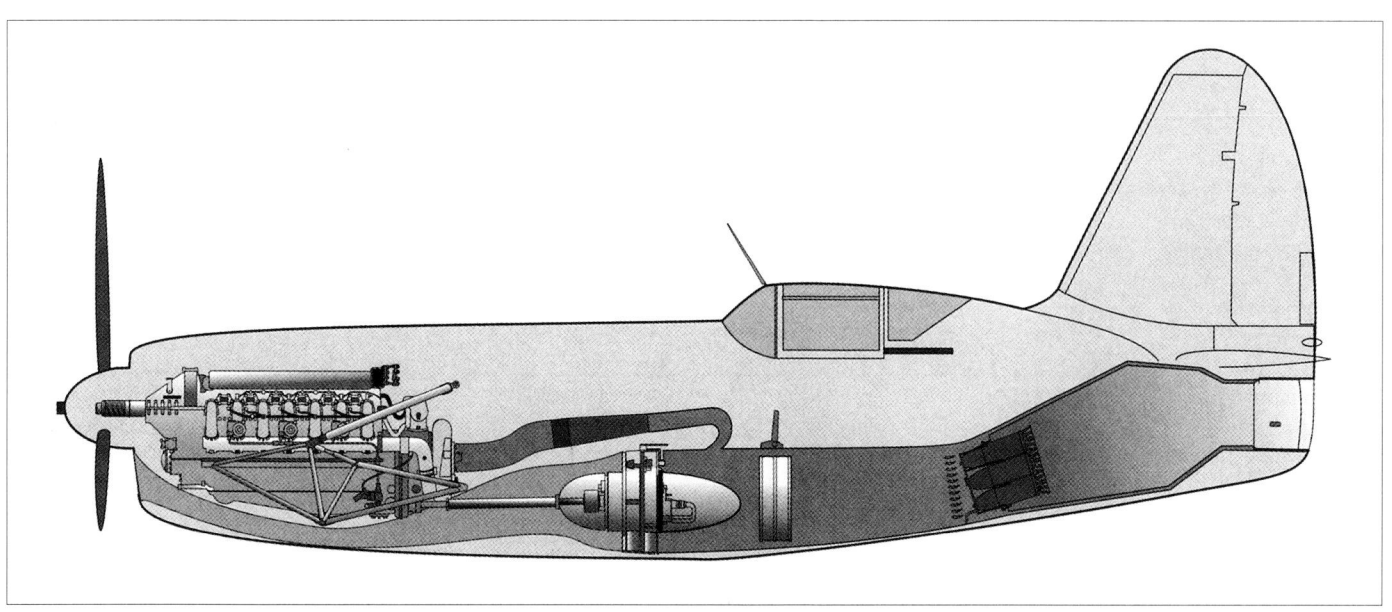

A schematic layout of the I-250 fighter's powerplant, showing the compressor of the VRDK booster driven via an extension shaft, with the water radiator behind it and the combustion chamber further aft. Note the auxiliary air duct running forward from the compressor to the main engine's supercharger.

95

Above and below: The prototype of the I-250 (c/n 01) as originally flown. Note the peculiar design of the levered suspension main gear units featuring leading arms. The aircraft was painted light grey overall.

Above and below: Soon after the beginning of flight tests I-250 c/n 01 was fitted with a redesigned fin of increased area to improve directional stability (compare this to the photos on page 96). The reduced distance from cockpit to fin and the increased distance between the star and the fin leading edge are clearly visible.

Above: Another view of the modified prototype during trials.
Below: This aspect of the I-250 illustrates the variable-nozzle eyelids of the VRDK booster and the oil cooler flow adjustment flaps just aft of the propeller.

and ignited by seven spark plugs. At this stage the duct expanded to form a combustion chamber fabricated from welded stainless steel to withstand the intense heat and corrosion generated by the combustion process.

Fortunately MiG had already been asked by NKAP in January 1944 to start preliminary work on this aircraft, known internally as type 'N' and externally as I-250. By 13th April specifications were outlined and agreed by the head of NII VVS, Lieutenant General P. A. Losukov and accepted on 22nd May by the chief engineer of the VVS, Colonel General A. K. Repin. It was Repin who commented that a high-altitude interceptor does not need the same protection for the pilot as a Shturmovik (attack aircraft) and proceeded to reduce the proposed full armoured protection for the pilot to a bulletproof glass windscreen and an armour plate for the back of the seat, the headrest and left arm. On 28th May 1944 NKAP instructed MiG to produce two prototypes of an all-metal high-altitude interceptor for the PVO and have them available for testing in February and March 1945. Essential performance characteristics included the ability to climb to 5,000 m (16,400 ft) in 4.5 minutes on full power and 5.5 minutes using only the piston engine, a top speed of 810 km/h (502 mph) at 7,000 m (23,000 ft) reduced to 700 km/h without the VRDK, and a service ceiling of 12,000 m (39,400 ft) with both engines and 11,000 m (36,100 m) with the piston engine only. Intended armament was one 23-mm cannon and two 12.7-mm machine-guns. TsAGI was detailed not only to provide assistance with aerodynamic and stress calculations but also to test a full-size mock-up in their wind tunnel within one month. TsIAM was charged with delivering three VRDK engines with 900 kg (1,990 lb) thrust at 7,000 m (23,000 ft) and 800 km/h (496 mph), with a fuel consumption of 1,200 kg/hr (2,652 lb/hr).

In the same NKAP order instructions were also given to Sukhoi's OKB to build a similar fighter to be called Su-5; this was in addition to fitting an RD-1KhZ rocket motor to the Su-6, which would then become the first (but not the only) Sukhoi aircraft to be designated Su-7. Yakovlev's OKB was to fit an RD-1KhZ rocket motor to a Yak-3 then add a three-chamber version of this rocket engine to another airframe. Lavochkin's OKB was to install an RD-1KhZ in an La-7 in addition to designing a fighter with Lyul'ka turbojets. Finally, Polikarpov's OKB was to produce a fighter with a two-chamber rocket motor. The Soviet authorities were determined to catch up with the developments in Western Europe.

On 19th September 1944 NKAP approved the preliminary specifications of the I-250 including a 3,500-kg (7,735-lb) take-off weight, a top speed of 825 km/h (512 mph) and climb to 5,000 m (16,400 ft) in 3.9 minutes. Shortly afterwards the VVS requested that a mock-up be constructed as soon as possible. On 26th October it was inspected by the State mock-up review commission but rejected because of the poor cockpit layout. However, since the fuselage of the first prototype was nearly finished and changes would have delayed completion, the mock-up was finally passed. There remained one or two modifications to be made as soon as possible, the most notable being the relocation of instruments.

In October 1944 the combustion chamber was sent to TsIAM for testing and a two-hour run showed the need for it to be strengthened. After this was done the modified chamber was tested until 17th November when the desired thrust was obtained. During December the complete powerplant was tested but the drive shaft between the two engines failed several times, necessitating design changes.

During December work continued on assembling the first prototype at OKB-155; meanwhile, a second fuselage was assembled for testing in the TsAGI wind tunnel and TsIAM completed the tests and modifications to the VRDK. The first prototype was completed on 26th February 1945 and, although the powerplant was still not ready, one change that could be initiated was a new type of propeller, the 3.1-m (10ft 2-in) diameter AV-10P-60 with the latest TsAGI VS-9 blade profile.

I-250 c/n 01 was ready for factory tests on 15th March 1945 and the first flight took place on 4th April (some sources suggest it was 3rd March) with test pilot A. P. Deyev at the controls. On 8th April, its third flight, the VRDK was tested in a dive and a speed of 710 km/h (440 mph) at 5,000 m (16,400 ft) was attained, but after landing a leak was found in the oil cooler, necessitating its return to *zavod* No.124 for repairs. Flying continued without the use of the VRDK which, when returned, was used again on 14th April but still gave trouble. However, encouragement was taken from reaching 809 km/h (502 mph) at about 7,000 m (23,000 ft) on 13th and 19th May, and also by the completion on the 19th of the second prototype sporting a smart blue colour scheme with a red and yellow fuselage flash.

Early test flights revealed unsatisfactory directional stability. Photos show that the vertical tail chord of I-250 c/n 01 was increased to remedy this but, curiously, no documentary proof of it has been found. By 30th May the VRDK of I-250 c/n 01 had run out of hours and was returned to TsIAM. Unfortunately, the third unit ordered was not ready and further tests had to be postponed.

On 26th May 1945 A. P. Deyev flew I-250 c/n 02 on its maiden flight. Later, several serious defects were discovered, including an oil leak from the compressor's sleeve. It was deemed necessary to bring in K. V. Kholshchevnikov to solve the problems. After the compressor had been repaired at TsIAM an attempt was made to take-off on 6th June but a sudden rise in oil temperature caused the flight to be aborted. Examination of the fuel filter revealed metallic swarf. The following day the M-107R failed with broken bearings and the entire powerplant was returned to TsIAM. A new power unit was installed and No.2 was airworthy again on the 29th June.

Meanwhile, I-250 c/n 01 was grounded again from 9th to 27th June for measures to remedy magneto trouble and the addition of extra air intakes to cool the spark plugs. Success on 3rd July resulted in a speed of 820 km/h (508 mph) at 6,700 m (22,000 ft), but this was followed by tragedy two days later. On the first prototype's 26th flight the port tailplane failed at low altitude and the fighter crashed; A. P. Deyev baled out but was killed because his parachute could not deploy in time. The cause of the crash was traced to manoeuvring at too high a g-load.

Undeterred by this accident, the authorities, who now took the view that future fighters would be powered only by jet engines, nonetheless decided it would be a good idea to train a cadre of pilots on high-speed flight in mixed-power aircraft to facilitate the changeover. To this end they decided that Suhkoi Su-5 development should be terminated as it was judged to be inferior to the I-250 of which a pre-production batch of ten was ordered on 27th July 1945.

Meanwhile, the tailplane of No.2 was belatedly strengthened and on receiving its repaired powerplant the fighter resumed flying on 20th July, piloted by A. P. Yakimov. Excess torque pulling to starboard was experienced which, the pilot said, made the aircraft too dangerous to fly; hence vertical tail area was enlarged again by 0.63 m² (6.8 sq.ft). The aircraft flew again on 14th August but the problem persisted, so this time the fin was given a 1° bias. Another test pilot, A. N. Chernoboorov joined the factory tests in September, completing them in January 1946 after many more incidents. It was subsequently decided not to send the I-250 for State acceptance trials before more development work was carried out on the powerplant, even though a pre-production batch of the aircraft had already been ordered. Trials continued with I-250 c/n 02 until 12th July 1946 when an engine fire resulted in a forced landing at Lyubertsy airfield and the aircraft was damaged beyond repair.

The order for ten I-250s had been placed with *zavod* No.381 (also located at Khodynka); the first two were to be completed in September 1945, the next three in October and the rest by the end of the year. This factory originated in Leningrad as 'Lenmetallurgstroi'

Above and below: The second prototype I-250 (c/n 02) differed outwardly in that it lacked the teardrop fairing under the VRDK booster nozzle, the tailwheel being housed completely within the rear fuselage. Note that the vertical tail has been enlarged again. The aircraft was blue overall with a red flash outlined in yellow.

Front and rear views of the second prototype I-250 (c/n 02). The narrow landing gear track is readily apparent. The I-250 was the first Mikoyan aircraft to feature wheel well doors which opened only when the landing gear was in transit.

The compressor and drive shaft of the Kholshchevnikov VRDK booster. Note the turbosupercharger at the back of the M-107R engine; the orifice is the air inlet.

and was taken over by NKAP on 12th August 1940 to make IL-2 components and numbered 381. It was evacuated to Nizhniy Tagil in September 1941 but never really settled down, although a few La-5s were built there; on 12th March 1943 it was converted into a tank diesel engine plant, the aircraft manufacturing equipment transferring to Khodynka. Here the plant thrived, repairing aircraft and building La-7s, for which it earned the Order of the Red Banner. Unfortunately manufacturing the I-250 was a much more complex task than had been appreciated. The plant was also struggling with another current order for five La-150 jet fighters; the target of producing ten I-250s before 31st December 1945 was realised to be hopelessly unrealistic and the programme was changed to building only one before the end of the year.

Although the airframe was completed the engine was not available in time. Criticism was piled upon the factory management, not all of it deserved because power cuts and a shortage of fuel for winter heating also contributed to their woes. However, one of the biggest problems was the constant changing of design drawings and specifications to remedy faults continually being discovered. The factory was attempting to mass-produce an ever-changing design. Furthermore, many of the delays and faults with engines and other out-sourced components were unfairly blamed on *zavod* No.381 as the ultimate supplier.

Aleksey I. Shakhoorin, who had been head of NKAP since 10th January 1940 and the Ministry of Aircraft Industry (MAP, *Ministerstvo aviatsionnoy promyshlennosti*) from its formation on 9th May 1945, was arrested and replaced by Mikhail V. Khrunichev in March 1946. On 13th April the new Minister severely reprimanded three aero engine factory directors and others, including K. V. Kholshchevnikov, and proceeded to set up a commission on 30th April to discover why *zavod* No.381 and TsIAM had failed to meet their I-250 deadlines. In the meantime, on 26th February the order for MiG-13s, as the I-250 was sometimes called, was increased to 50 and yet it still had not begun its State acceptance trials. When the commission reported its findings, which spread the blame fairly evenly along the chain of command, the new Minister refused to accept them and placed the major part of the blame firmly at the feet of V. I. Zhuravlyov, Director of *zavod* No.381. Consequently, both Zhuravlyov and his Quality Control Manager were sacked and arrested for industrial sabotage.

A new deadline for the delivery of the first series-produced I-250 was set at 5th July 1946 but not achieved and 24-hour shifts were imposed – only for the next deadline to be stymied by VRDK engine delivery problems. By this time seven airframes had been completed and were awaiting engines. The first production aircraft (c/n 3810108 – ie, 8th aircraft from the 1st batch built by *zavod* No.381); to be accepted by OKB-155 was delivered on 8th August. 1946 Its first flight with I. T. Ivashchenko at the controls took place three days later, during which exhaust seals failed and a number of ignition cables were scorched – fortunately without triggering a crash.

A delay in repairing the aircraft and replacing the engine resulted in the I-250 missing its planned appearance at the Tushino Air Display. It finally arrived at GK NII VVS for State acceptance trials on 15th September with V. N. Sorokin appointed as chief engineer and I. T. Ivashchenko as test pilot. Once again the tests had to be delayed – this time by instructions from Stalin that nine I-250s, together with the latest jet aircraft, should participate in the flypast over the Kremlin on 7th November to celebrate the October Revolution anniversary. (The anomaly with the dates is explained by the discrepancy between the old and the Gregorian calendar, which was not adopted until after the formation of the USSR.)

On 30th October 1946 eight I-250s (c/ns 3810101 to 3810106, 3810108 and 3810109) were delivered to the VVS; aircraft No. 3810107 was for static structural tests and aircraft No.3810110 for static engine tests. By this time the VK-107R-plus-VRDK combination had been designated E-30-20. Great care was taken to select only the ten most competent pilots from the 176th *Proskoorovskiy* GvIAP of the 324th IAD PVO. This regiment went on to become the famous 234th GvIAP which now contains the two renowned aerobatic teams, the **Roos**skiye **Vit**yazi (Russian Knights) and *Stri**zhi*** (Swifts). Training was extremely thorough and in addition to flying the I-250 each pilot received 114 hours of lectures on engineering and flying techniques. After a tremendous effort the aircraft and pilots were ready but bad weather caused the flypast to be cancelled. At least Muscovites were spared the ear-splitting roar generated by nine I-250s with VRDK engines at full blast.

An important meeting chaired by Stalin took place on 29th November 1946 when future policy on jet fighters for the VVS and PVO was determined. For the principal type of fighter the MiG-9 (the jet-powered one) was selected, with the Yak-15 used for pilot familiarisation on jet aircraft and conversion training. The La-150 was afforded more time for improvements but production of the I-250 was to cease. With the prospect of reliable jet engines being procured from Great Britain and help available from German engineers, it was decided that there was no longer a future for mixed-power fighters. However, Stalin insisted that the I-250 must complete its State acceptance trials and that all jigs and drawings should be retained, together with the unassembled parts, which amounted to nearly 90% of a complete aircraft.

State acceptance trials were only possible after completion of similar tests by its engine, the VRDK, which was not to be until May 1947. Because the VVS was no longer interested in this fighter there was an attempt to persuade the naval air arm, VVS VMF (VVS *Voyenno-morskovo flota*), to use the I-250 as an escort fighter for torpedo bombers. To this end extra fuel tanks were installed in the wings and fuselage of I-250 c/n 3810102 to carry an additional 218 litres (48 Imp. gal.) of fuel and oil tank capacity was increased to 78 litres (17 Imp. gal.). It was therefore considered appropriate that the State acceptance trials should be conducted at the NII VVS VMF airfield at Skul'te, near Riga, and so 3810102 was flown there to start tests on 9th October. Bad weather and reliability problems ensured that by 21st January 1948 only six flights totalling 2 hours 25 minutes had been completed; furthermore, the VRDK unit had been engaged only once, and then for only 1.5 minutes on a ground run. Unsurprisingly, on 3rd April 1948 the I-250 was officially announced to have failed its State acceptance trials and the VVS VMF lost all interest in the aircraft. Official documents dated May 1948 refer to the formal withdrawal from service of the I-250, presumably alluding to the machines received by the VVS for the 1946 flypast, although there is no record of either the VVS or the VVS VMF operating any I-250s. It is probably no coincidence that the prototype of the world-beating MiG-15 had completed its factory trials on 25th March 1948 and that *zavod* No.1 *imeni Stalina* in Kuibyshev was instructed in May to begin preparations for its production.

Structural description of the I-250

The I-250 was a low-wing all-metal monoplane with a long nose and a radiator under the propeller spinner endowing it with a pugnacious profile which was further accen-

The M-107R engine with the cowling removed, showing the ammunition boxes aft of the engine and the air duct for the VRDK underneath.

103

Above and below: I-250 (MiG-13) c/n 3810102 at the Naval Air Arm Research Institute (NII AV VMF) at Riga-Skul'te. Note the taller vertical tail characteristic of production aircraft (the area had to be increased yet again), the cannon muzzle openings and the 'anti-soot' stripe aft of the exhaust stubs.

Above and below: Two more views of the same aircraft during State acceptance trials. The strong wing dihedral is seen to good effect.

Rear view of I-250 c/n 3810102. Note that the aerial mast on top of the windscreen is canted to starboard.

tuated by the short fuselage with the cockpit placed well aft. As usual, the fuselage was in three sections and had an all-metal stressed-skin construction with the front section having a structure of chromium-manganese steel alloy tubes carrying the main engine and guns. The middle section had a riveted construction with pressed bulkheads joined by four sheet steel longerons with duralumin stringers, cabin floor and skin panels. To carry the VRDK compressor its bulkhead was cast steel and the section ended with a steel bulkhead supporting the combustion chamber. The bulkheads of the monocoque tail section were made of pressed duralumin, except for the final one of welded steel carrying the jet nozzle. The rear structure also had longerons, stringers and skin panels of duralumin.

To reduce the temperature of the combustion chamber walls and protect the fuselage, water from a 78-litre (17-Imp. gal.) tank was sprayed over the duct, with the added bonus that the steam augmented thrust. The accelerating jet of high-velocity gases exited through hydraulically controlled nozzle eyelids which, in cruise flight, faired over the nozzle to reduce drag. It was estimated that at 7,000 m (23,000 ft) the total engine system produced 2,500 hp, of which 1,350 hp originated from the booster. Careful positioning of the soft cellular self-sealing fuel tanks away from hot spots reduced fire hazards. Two tanks, each holding 90 litres (20 Imp. gal.), were in the wing centre section with a third, of 390 litres (86 Imp. gal.), located in front of the cockpit which then had to be positioned well aft in the manner of the MiG-3.

To counter the propeller torque which tried to veer the aircraft to starboard the rudder was angled at 1° 20' and the horizontal tail had a NACA 0009 aerofoil. The tail section had a duralumin structure with a magnesium alloy skin.

The single-spar wings of tapered planform and 7° dihedral were given a main beam with steel flanges and duralumin web, stringers and ribs (except those carrying the undercarriage, which were made of steel). Wing thickness was 12% chord at roots and 10% at the tips with a TsAGI 1A10 aerofoil section at the roots tapering to 1B10 at the tips. Frise ailerons, TsAGI slotted flaps plus small Schrenk type flaps under the wing roots comprised the wing control surfaces, all of which had duralumin structures and magnesium alloy skins.

A feature of the main landing gear was that the levered-suspension arms carrying the wheels were ahead of the legs to ensure that the wheel well doors were closed at all times except when the gear was retracting or descending. The mainwheel tyres were 650 x 250 mm (25.5 x 9.84 in) and there was a 170 x 100 mm (6.69 x 3.9 in) castoring tailwheel which retracted into a fairing under the jet nozzle and which the pilot could lock neutral when down.

The cockpit canopy had an armoured glass windscreen with 6-mm (0.23-in) thick Perspex panels which slid back for access and another armoured glass panel at the back. Behind the seat were an RSI-6MU receiver and an RSI-3M1 transmitter. The VRDK engine was controlled by two levers on the port side console and operable in all flight modes except climb and take-off. Changes of speed in the two-speed compressor were automatic.

The armament had been improved since the original specification and comprised two synchronised 20-mm Berezin B-20 cannon on the engine's flanks plus a third firing through the propeller hub. Each cannon had 100 rounds, later increased to 160, and was aimed through a PBP-1A gunsight.

Take-off was slow and difficult due to the extra weight of the VRDK engine, which could not be used in this mode. Taxying visibility was poor and there was a strong tendency to veer to starboard, which could not be fully countered by the rudder, necessitating braking. Operating the jet booster was an additional task for the pilot who was nearly deafened by its noise. Control response was criticised, as were the arrangement of the instruments, the transparency of the hood, poor manoeuvrability and difficulty of maintenance. Undoubtedly only highly skilled pilots could fly the I-250. Its redeeming features were its heavy armament and a top speed that was over 100 km/h (62 mph) faster than that of other piston-engined fighters in service with the VVS. Unfortunately, speed depended on the VRDK unit which was not only unreliable but had a short TBO (time between overhauls); this had started at an unacceptable 10 hours but subsequently rose to 35 hours.

Details and performance data of the I-250:

	Prototype (c/n 01)	C/n 3810102
Span	9.5 m (31 ft 2 in)	9.5 m (31 ft 2 in)
Length	8.19 m (26 ft 10½ in)	8.19 m (26 ft 10½ in)
Wing area, m² (sq.ft)	15 (162)	15 (162)
Weight empty, kg (lb)	2,797 (6,181)	3,028 (6,692)
Take-off weight, kg (lb)	3,680 (8,133)	3,931 (8,688)
Wing loading, kg/m² (lb/sq.ft)	245 (50)	262 (54)
Top speed at sea level with VRDK, km/h (mph)	680 (422)	n.a.
Top speed with VRDK, km/h (mph)	820 (508)	n.a.
at altitude, m (ft)	6,600 (21,600)	n.a.
Service ceiling (estimated), m (ft)	11,900 (39,000)	n.a.
Range (estimated), km (miles)	790 (490)	n.a.
Take-off run, m (ft)	n.a.	800 (2,620)
Landing run, m (ft)	n.a.	1,000 (3,280)
Landing speed, km/h (mph)	n.a.	195 (121)

Chapter 8

The First Mikoyan Twin

DIS-200 (MiG-5, Type 'T', *izdeliye* 71)

As the MiG-1 was starting to roll off the production lines of zavod No.1, its OKO was asked by NKAP on 7th October 1940 to start work on a twin-engined, long-range, single-seat escort fighter to be designated DIS-200 (*dvookhmotornyy istrebitel' soprovozhdeniya*, twin-engined escort fighter). The need for this was made clear to the VVS staff the previous year when RAF Bomber Command sustained unacceptably heavy losses while attempting daylight raids on Germany with unescorted bombers and was forced to switch to night attacks in which the likelihood of hitting the target was reduced. NKAP asked the OKO to prepare design specifications for such a fighter with Mikulin AM-37 engines, together with a display model, for presentation to its officials on 12th November 1940.

Having successfully presented their proposals, the OKO was gratified to learn that the DIS-200 was included in the 1941 plan for experimental aircraft approved by the government on 25th November. Four days later the OKO was instructed to produce three prototypes ready for their State acceptance trials on 1st August, 1st September and 1st November 1941 respectively. By this time the aircraft's role had been extended to include bombing, torpedo attack, reconnaissance and interdiction. Great emphasis was placed on long range and the ability to perform combat patrols over enemy territory.

On 2nd October 1940 NKAP instructed that after completion of State acceptance trials zavod No.1 was to transfer some of its production of the MiG-1 to zavod No.21 *imeni* G. K. Ordzhonikidze and start building the DIS-200 as the MiG-5. Within the OKO the aircraft was known as type 'T' and in the factory as *izdeliye* 71; it has also been suggested that the bomber version, if series-produced, would have been designated MiG-2.

According to an NKAP order of 11th March 1941, manufacturer's flight tests of the DIS-200 were to be conducted by chief engineer A. G. Broonov and test pilot A. N. Yekatov. However, A. I. Zhookov replaced the latter in accordance with another order dated 13th May 1941.

The first flight of the DIS-200 took place on 11th June 1941 with A. I. Zhookov at the controls. Factory tests started on 1st July at LII NKAP and were completed on 5th October.

This view of the first prototype DIS-200 (T) escort fighter shows the exhaust stains on the wing upper surface and the oil cooler outlets outboard of the engine nacelles.

With AV-5L-114 three-blade propellers of 3.1 m (10 ft 2 in) diameter, the top speed at 7,500 m (24,600 ft) was 560 km/h (347 mph) – a disappointing 104 km/h (64 mph) slower than predicted. While four-blade AV-9B-L-149 propellers of 3.0 m (9 ft 10 in) diameter were being fitted, the opportunity was taken to redesign the exhaust manifolds, oil cooler and inlet branch pipes and to reposition the air exit tunnel from the oil cooler. Wind-tunnel tests on a scale model at TsAGI confirmed that poorly designed engine accessories were the cause of the extra drag. After these modifications maximum speed rose to 610 km/h (378 mph) at 6,800 m (22,300 ft) and a time of 5.5 minutes to climb to 5,000 m (16,400 ft) was recorded.

A low-wing monoplane with twin tails, the DIS-200 was designed with large components suitable for mass-production and ease of assembly. The fuselage comprised a duralumin front section, a wooden monocoque middle section and a rear section of steel tubular structure with duralumin panelled skin. The front section, bolted to both the front wing spar and the first frame of the wing centre section, was based on three stout beams which, together with their cross-members, formed the cockpit floor and also supported the bomb load and guns. In front of the cockpit the streamlined nose cone had a glass panel to afford downward visibility; the pilot also enjoyed a good all-round view above eye level thanks to a fully glazed canopy. For entering the cockpit the glazed panels were slid back and could be jettisoned for an emergency exit. With the exception of the two self-sealing fuel tanks and their supports, the middle section was all wood with a veneer skin. Four additional fuel tanks were in the wings and a total of 1,920 kg (4,243 lb) of fuel was carried. The all-metal fuselage tail section supported the wooden twin tail that had an electrically operated variable-incidence tailplane. The elevators had duralumin frames covered with fabric and on the port side was a trim tab, a feature that was also fitted to both rudders.

The wings had a Clark YH aerofoil section with a two-spar structure and a metal centre section. The outer wing panels connected to the centre section along the longerons were all wood, except for the fabric-covered ailerons and veneer-skin covered flaps, both of which had a duralumin frame. The Schrenk-type flaps were in two sections, one on the centre section and the other on the outer wings which also had automatic leading-edge slats covering two-thirds of its span. The ailerons were linked to deflect together through 20° when the flaps were lowered.

A pneumatically operated main undercarriage with 1,000 x 350 mm (39.3 x 13.77 in) wheels retracted backwards into the engine nacelles and a 470 x 210 mm (18.5 x 8.25 in) tailwheel retracted into the rear fuselage.

Above and below: These views of the DIS-200 (T) during manufacturer's tests show the slight inverted-gull shape of the wings, the water radiator intakes outboard of the engines and the similarity of the engine nacelles' design to the MiG-3's cowling shape.

Some sources indicate that it was originally intended to fit Charomskiy diesel engines, but they were not developed sufficiently at the time and so Mikulin AM-37 engines of 1,450 hp (1,044 kW) were underslung from the centre section with oil coolers outboard of them on the outer wing panels. Glycol was cooled in a radiator located behind the engine by air from a scoop on each side of the nacelle, discharging from it immediately below the wing trailing edge. The supercharger air inlets were in the outer wing leading edges and engine exhaust gases were collected on both sides of the engines into 'dog-leg' pipes to discharge over the top of the wings.

The powerful armament envisaged comprised one 23-mm Volkov/Yartsev VYa-23 cannon with about 200 rounds in a removable pod beneath the nose, two synchronised 12.7-mm Berezin UBS machine-guns with 300 rpg in the bottom of the centre section leading edge and four 7.62-mm ShKAS machine-guns with 1,000 rpg above them. However, the VVS preferred the Taubin MP-6 cannon, changing the specification to two MP-6s with 120 rpg; a bad move which ultimately proved a failure, necessitating a speedy reversion to the VYa-23. When required, the cannon pod could be removed and replaced by a bomb load of up to 1,000 kg (2,200 lb) or a torpedo. Consideration was also given to the installation of two aft-firing RO-82 unguided rocket launchers to protect the rear but this option was not pursued.

As a result of the disappointing performance in factory tests, LII recommended that series production be postponed but that development and tests continue in an effort to improve the design and this judgement was accepted by NKAP. However, Germany invaded the USSR on 22nd June 1941 and in October that year, with the enemy approaching the gates of Moscow, the institute and the DIS-200 were evacuated to Kazan' while the OKO and its factory went to Kuibyshev. All work on the DIS-200 with AM-37 engines was stopped in 1942 as a result of the failure of the AM-37 to reach series production. At that time the DIS-200 had three competitors for the escort fighter role: the Tairov Ta-3, Polikarpov TIS and Grooshin Gr-1. None of them progressed beyond the prototype stage; for this role the VVS used the Petlyakov Pe-3bis. It was wisely considered, in those troubled times, to accept a slightly inferior performance from an existing type suitably modified rather than lose any aircraft production whilst changing to a brand-new design.

DIS-200 with M-82 (Type 'IT', MiG-5)

The OKO designation type 'IT' was given to the second prototype of the DIS-200 built with Shvetsov M-82 14-cylinder radial engines rated at 1,700 hp (1,250 kW) for take-off and 1,300 hp (957 kW) at 6,500 m (21,300 ft). Two 3.2-m (10ft 6-in) diameter AV-9L-118 propellers were fitted and the tailcone modified to open out, forming an air brake. The only other change from the type 'T' specification was the armament which now comprised two 23-mm VYa-23 cannon, each with 150 rounds, in an undernose pod and four 12.7-mm UBK machine-guns, each with 250 rounds, in the leading edges of the wing centre section.

An NKAP order of 13th May 1941 had stopped production of the AM-35A in zavod 19 imeni Stalina, replacing it with the M-82. As the AM-37 still had not reached series production, all design teams were instructed by NKAP on 13th May 1941 to use the M-82 engine on their products. Although factory trials were scheduled to start on 25th September 1941, this target was not met and the evacuation of zavod No.1 and its OKO to Kuibyshev in October delayed its construction still further until autumn 1942.

An instruction on 4th June 1942 ordered factory trails to be conducted by chief test pilot G. M. Shiyanov and engineers Ootkin (LII) and V. N. Sorokin (OKO) but when the first flight finally took place on 28th January 1943 V. N. Savkin was the pilot, not Shiyanov.

Some sources have given January 1942 and even 15th October 1941 as the date of the first flight and this anomaly raises the possibility that there may have been *two* prototypes built with M-82 engines. This is corroborated by the fact that the initial order (25th September 1940) was for three examples of the DIS-200, followed on 10th May 1941 by another order for two with M-82 engines. However, given that the OKO and factory had just been evacuated and that priority was to build up production of types already on the lines, the suggestion of two prototypes with M-82 engines seems fanciful and a more plausible explanation is that the earlier dates were incorrect.

Another mystery is that there is a reference in RGAMO (*Rosseeyskiy gosoodarstvennyy arkhiv Ministerstva oborony* - Russian State Archive of Defence Ministry) f. 35 (NII VVS), op. 48576, d. 604, p. 8 to the State acceptance trials of type 'IT' starting on 27th January 1943 at LII, with the first flight on the following day. It was very unusual for State acceptance trials to start *before any factory tests have been conducted*. Perhaps the upheaval caused by the recent arrival of eight evacuated plants, including zavod No.1 from Moscow, onto an incomplete zavod No.122 site prompted the decision to transfer the first flight to the Flight Research Institute. Alternatively, it could have simply been a clerical error and the reference was in fact to factory tests.

The tests were disappointing, with a top speed of 604 km/h (374 mph) and a time to 5,000 m (16,400 ft) of 6.3 minutes, but further development was interrupted on 10th February 1943 by problems with the BP-82 floatless carburettors which had to be sent to TsIAM for adjustment. Carburettor problems continued to cause delays and priority for flight-testing was given to other aircraft. The engines were, however, eventually ground tested on 12th May but five months later, an instruction by NKAP stopped all further development and the propellers were sent to LII for use on other aircraft.

In spite of failing to propel a successor to the MiG-3 into mass-production during the war, the OKB of Mikoyan and Guryevich learned some valuable lessons designing and building high-altitude interceptor prototypes. The knowledge accumulated stood them in good stead when designing post-war jet fighters. After the modest success of the MiG-9 (the second to carry this designation) the OKB produced a succession of jet fighters as good as and for short periods of time, better in their class than anything else in the world.

Details and performance figures for the DIS-200:

Type	T	IT
Powerplant	2 x AM-37	2 x M-82
Span	15.3 m (50 ft 2¼ in)	15.3 m (50 ft 2¼ in)
Length	11.2 m (36 ft 7 in)	12.1 m (39 ft 8¼ in)
Wing area, m² (sq.ft)	38.9 (418.5)	38.9 (418.5)
Take-off weight, kg (lb)	8,060 (17,810)	8,000 (17,680)
Wing loading, kg/m² (lb/sq.ft)	207.2 (42.6)	205.7 (42.25)
Top speed, km/h (mph)	610 (378)	604 (374)
at altitude, m (ft)	6,800 (22,300)	Not recorded
Time to 5,000 m (16,400 ft), minutes	5.5	6.3
Service ceiling, m (ft)	10,900 (35,800)	9,800 (32,100)*
Range, km (miles)	2,280 (1,420)	2,500 (1,550)*

* Estimated

Above and below: The second prototype of the DIS-200 (also known as the IT) was powered by Shvetsov M-82 radials, which required the engine nacelles to be totally redesigned. Note also the extended split tailcone which opened to act as an airbrake.

Two more views of the DIS-200 (IT), showing the armament housed in the inner wings. With its bubble canopy and glazed underside of the extreme nose, the DIS-200 offered the pilot an unrestricted all-round view.

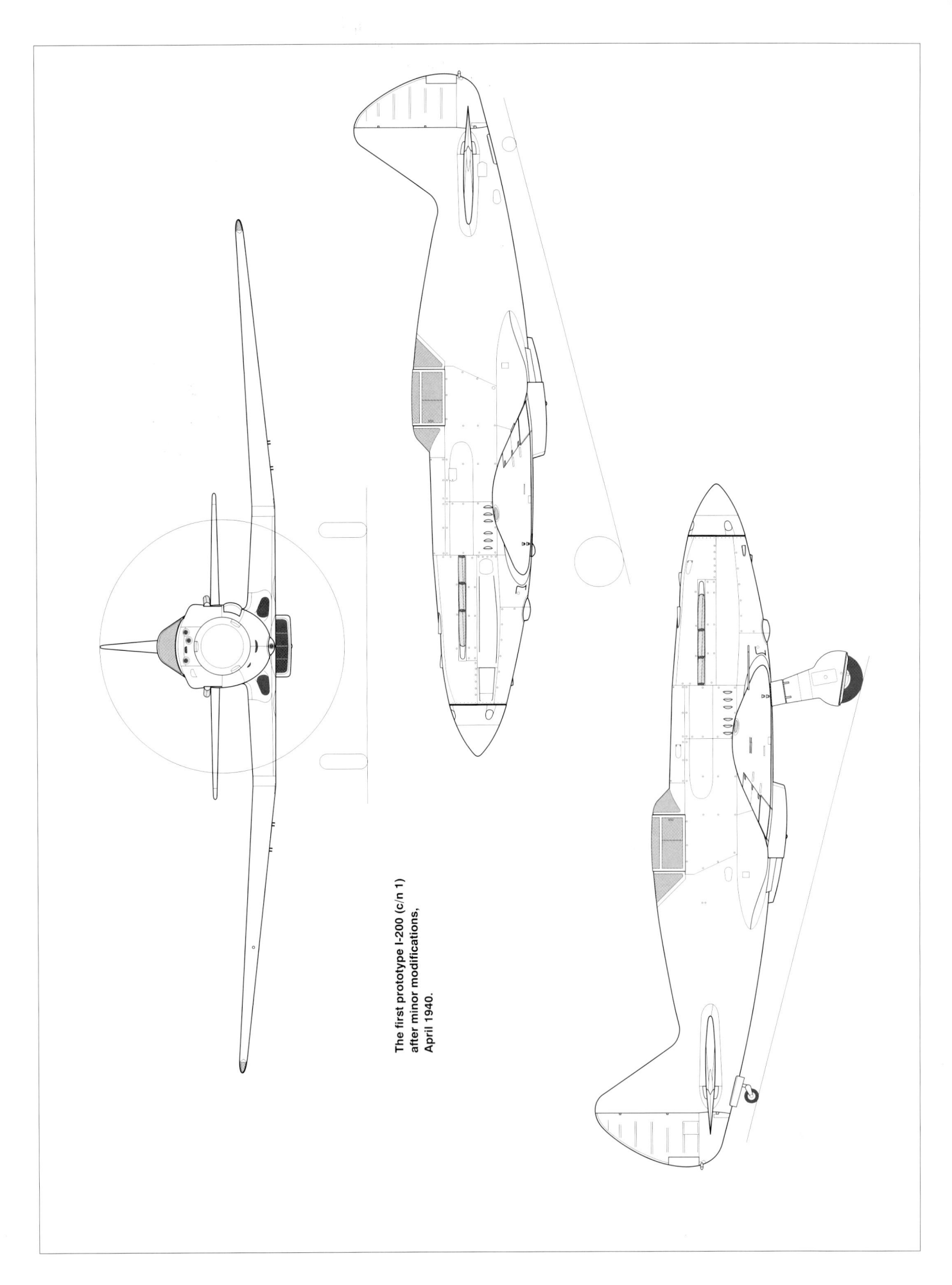

The first prototype I-200 (c/n 1) after minor modifications, April 1940.

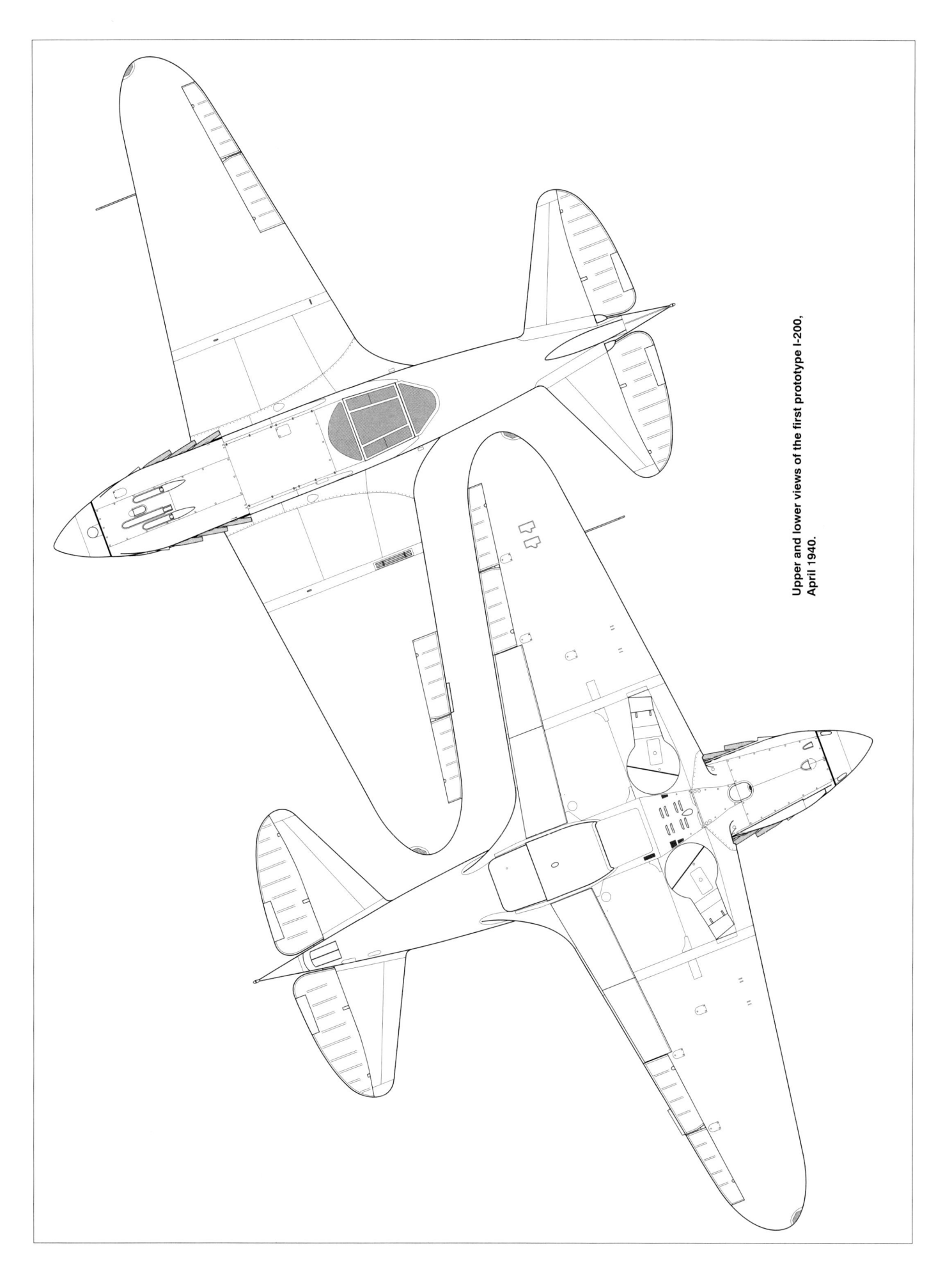

Upper and lower views of the first prototype I-200, April 1940.

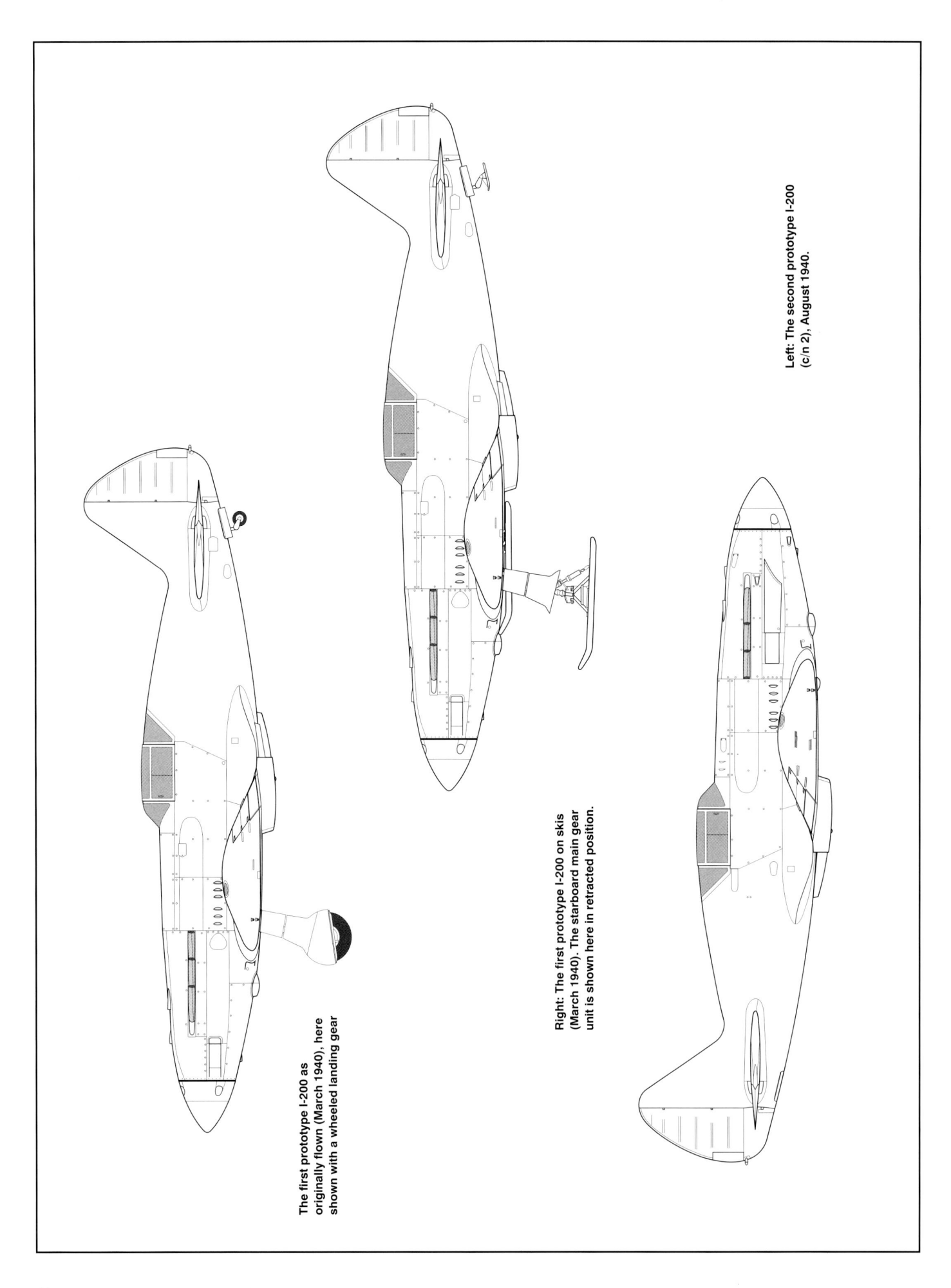

The first prototype I-200 as originally flown (March 1940), here shown with a wheeled landing gear

Right: The first prototype I-200 on skis (March 1940). The starboard main gear unit is shown here in retracted position.

Left: The second prototype I-200 (c/n 2), August 1940.

The third prototype I-200 (c/n 3), August 1940.

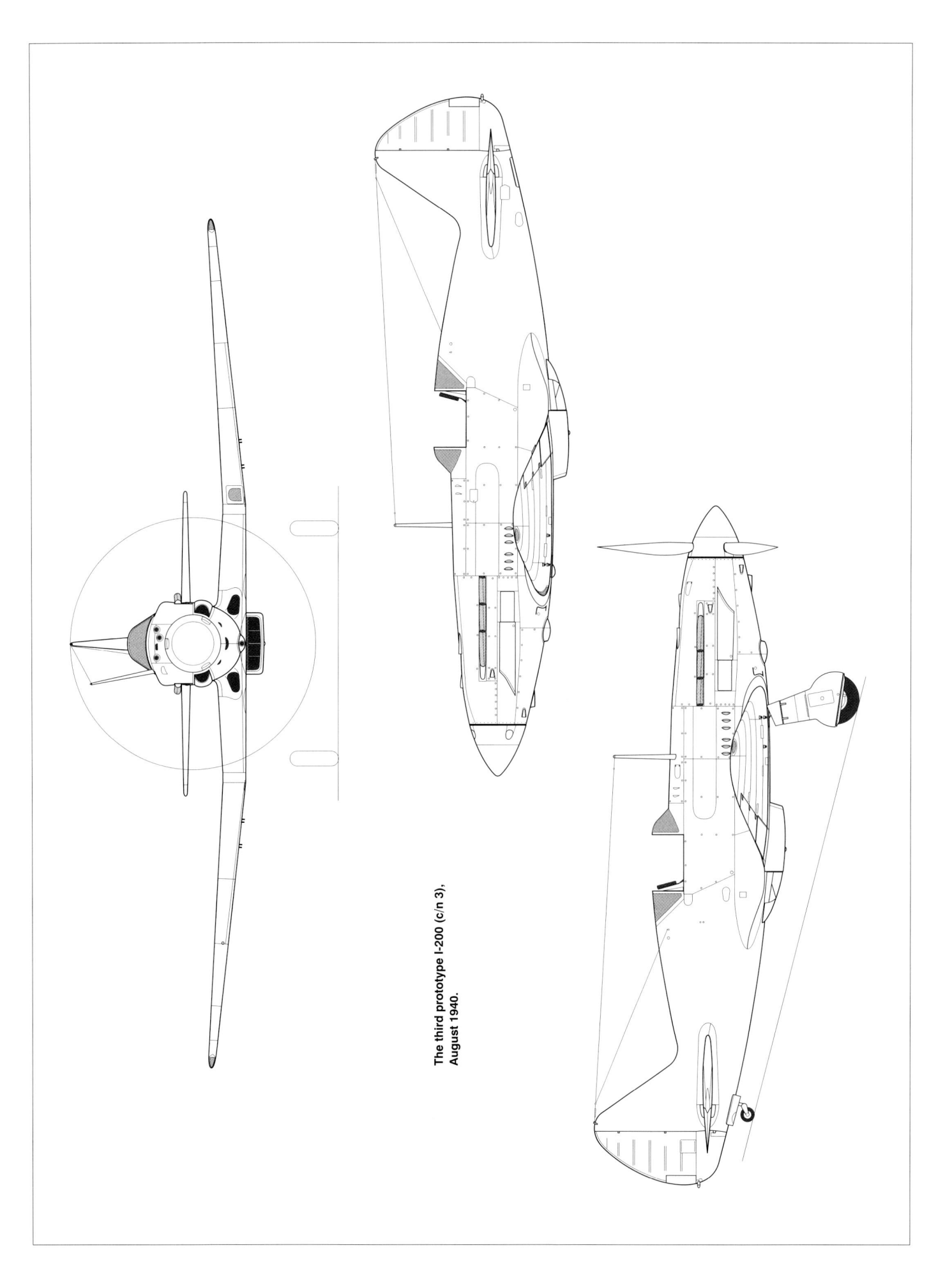

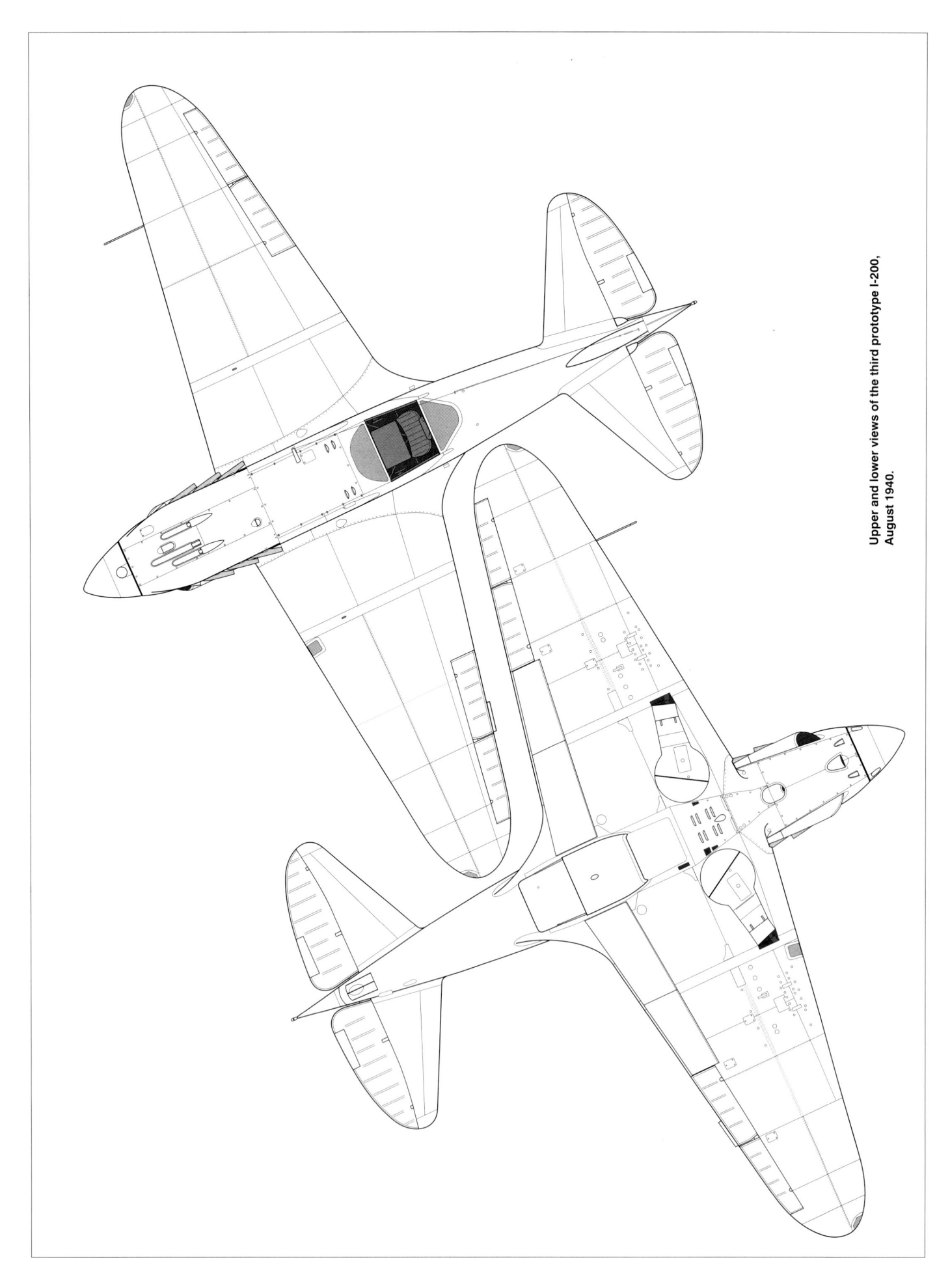

Upper and lower views of the third prototype I-200, August 1940.

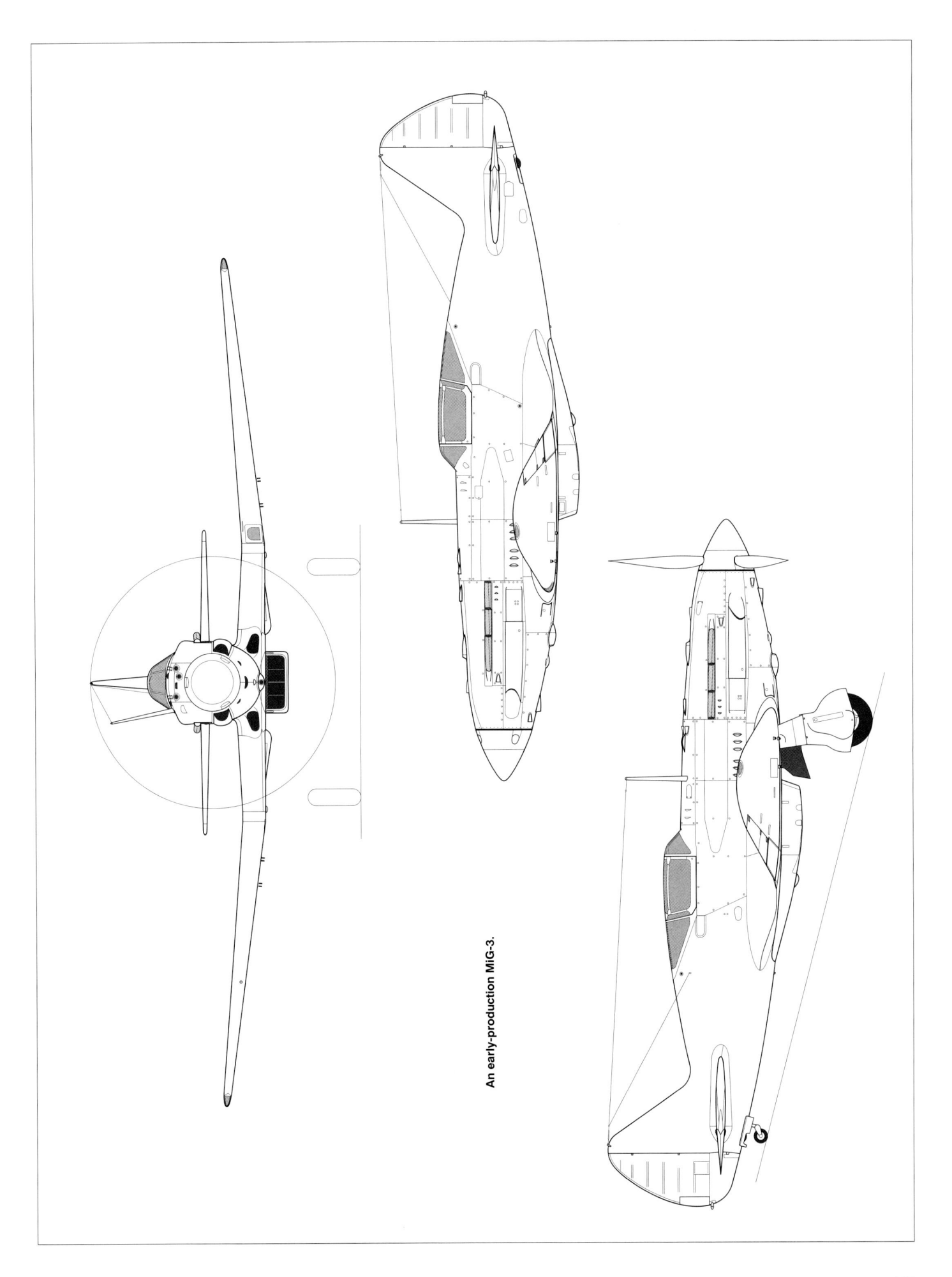

An early-production MiG-3.

117

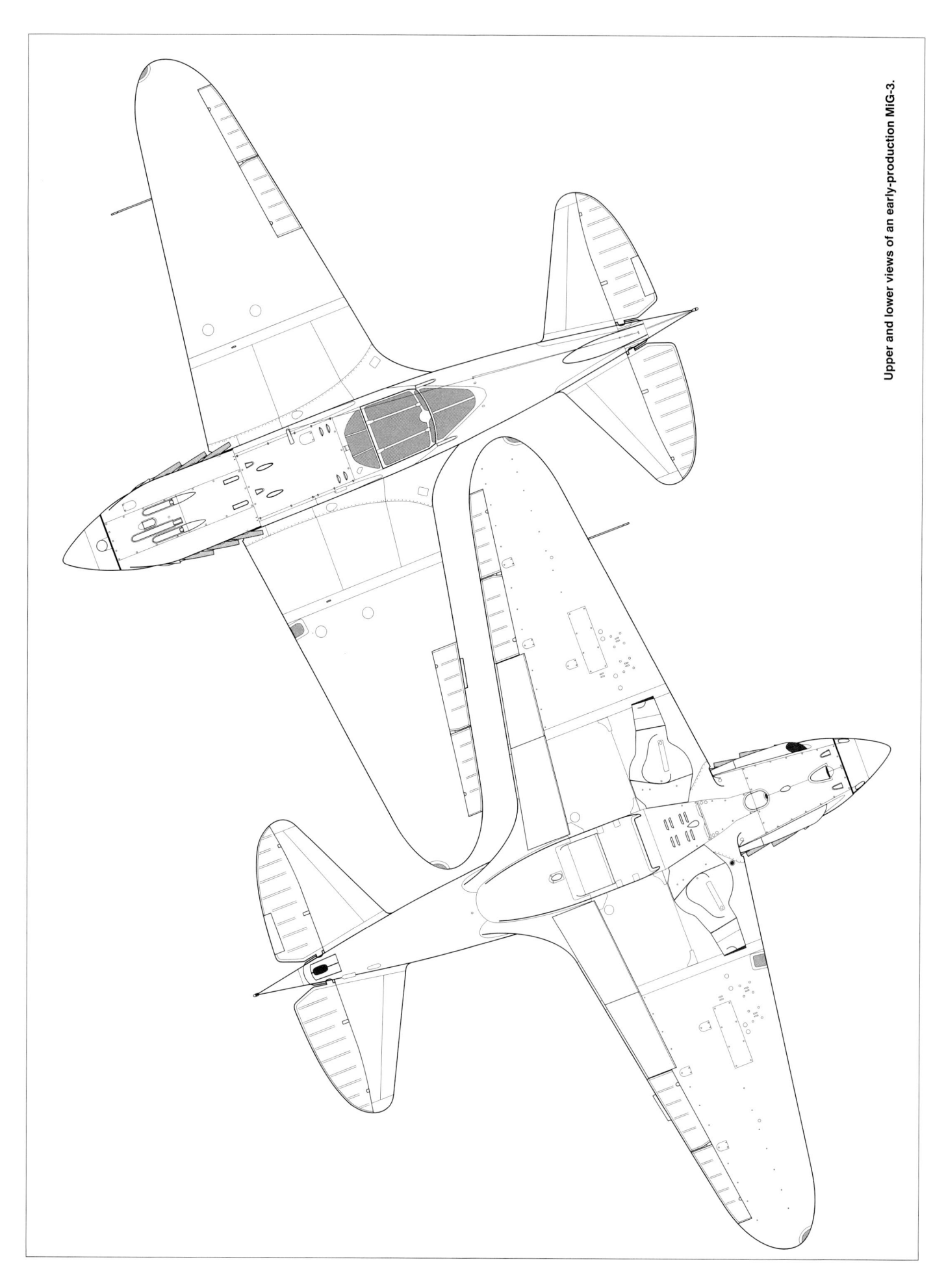

Upper and lower views of an early-production MiG-3.

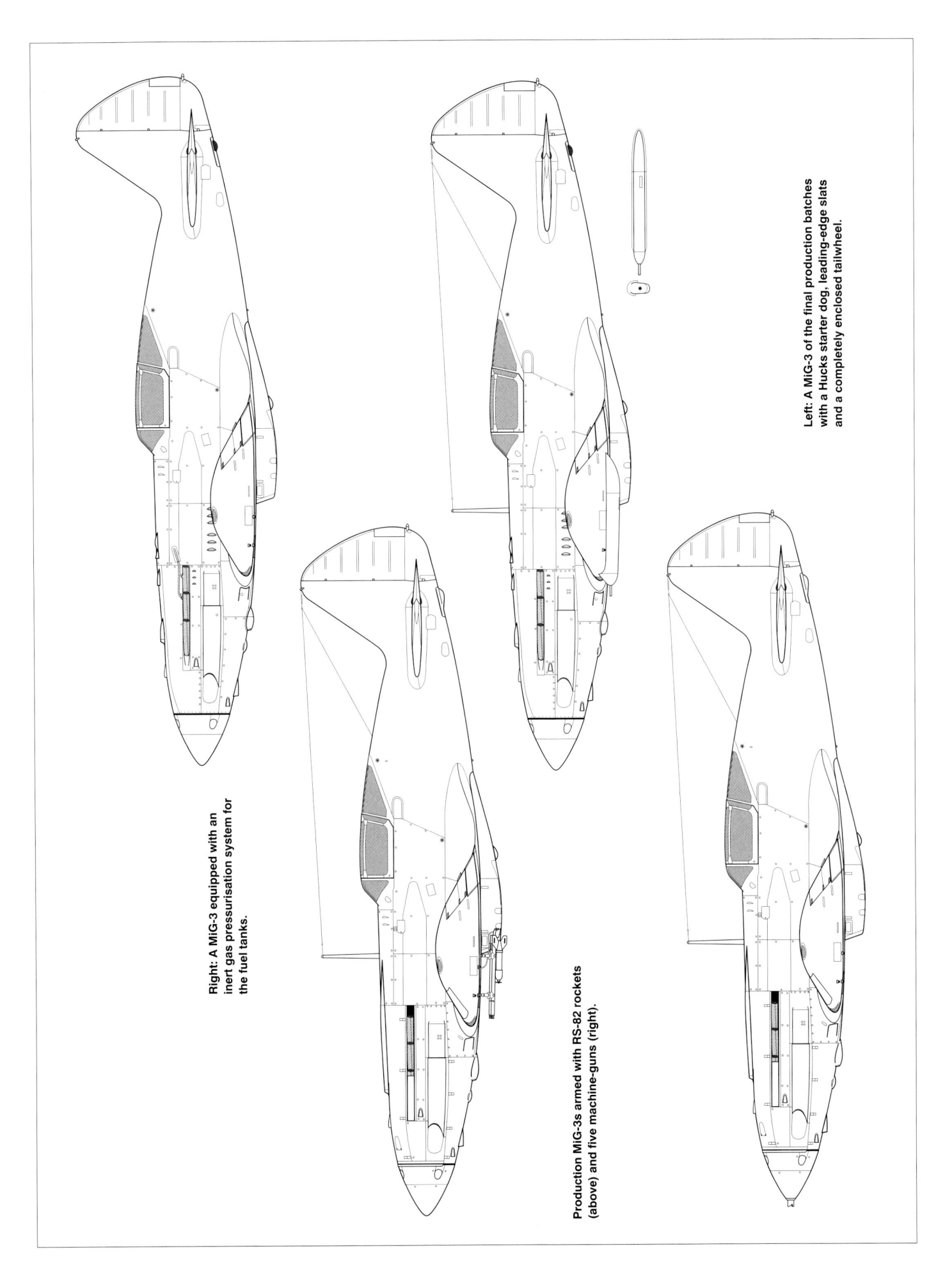

Right: A MiG-3 equipped with an inert gas pressurisation system for the fuel tanks.

Production MiG-3s armed with RS-82 rockets (above) and five machine-guns (right).

Left: A MiG-3 of the final production batches with a Hucks starter dog, leading-edge slats and a completely enclosed tailwheel.

119

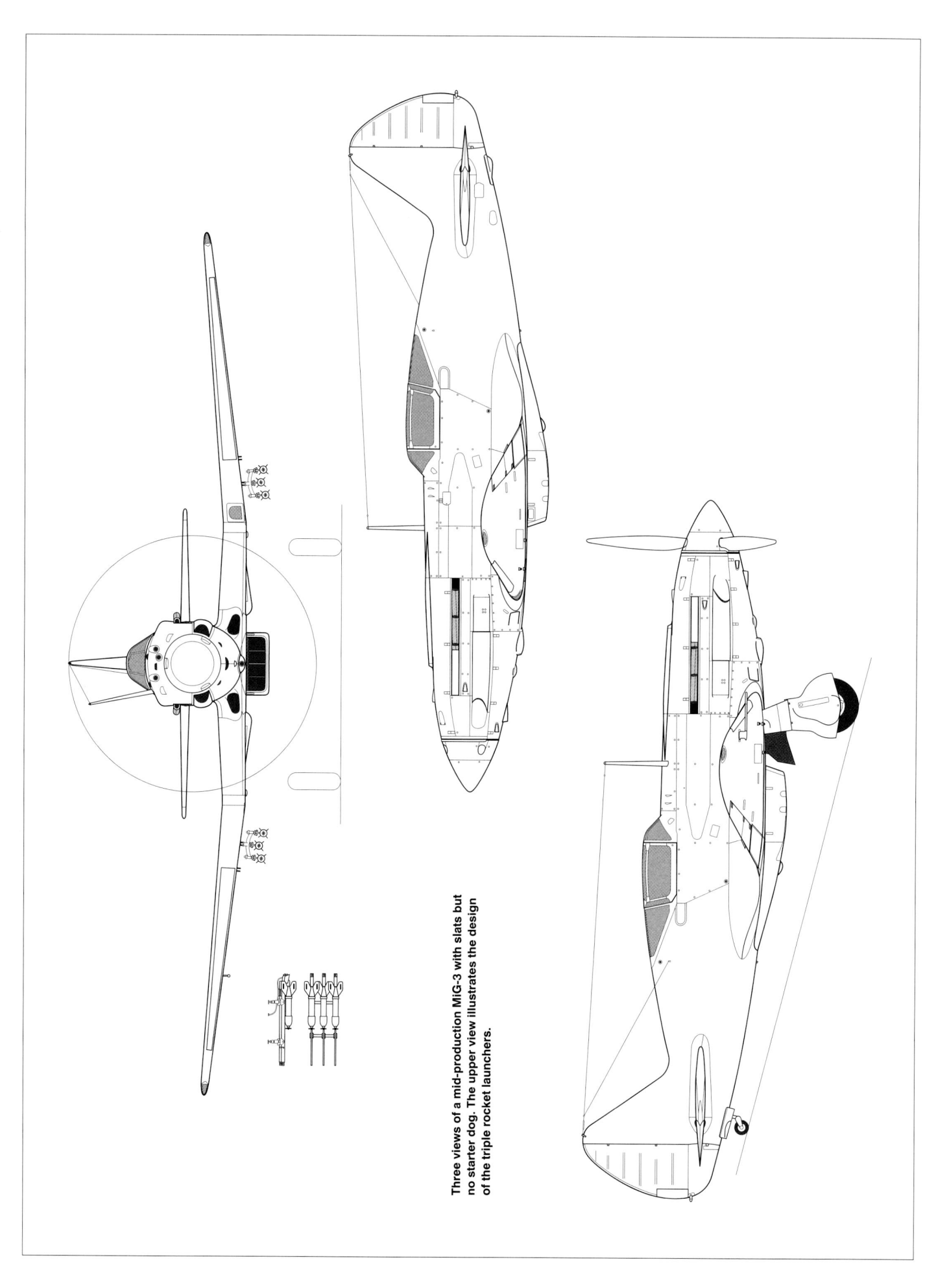

Three views of a mid-production MiG-3 with slats but no starter dog. The upper view illustrates the design of the triple rocket launchers.

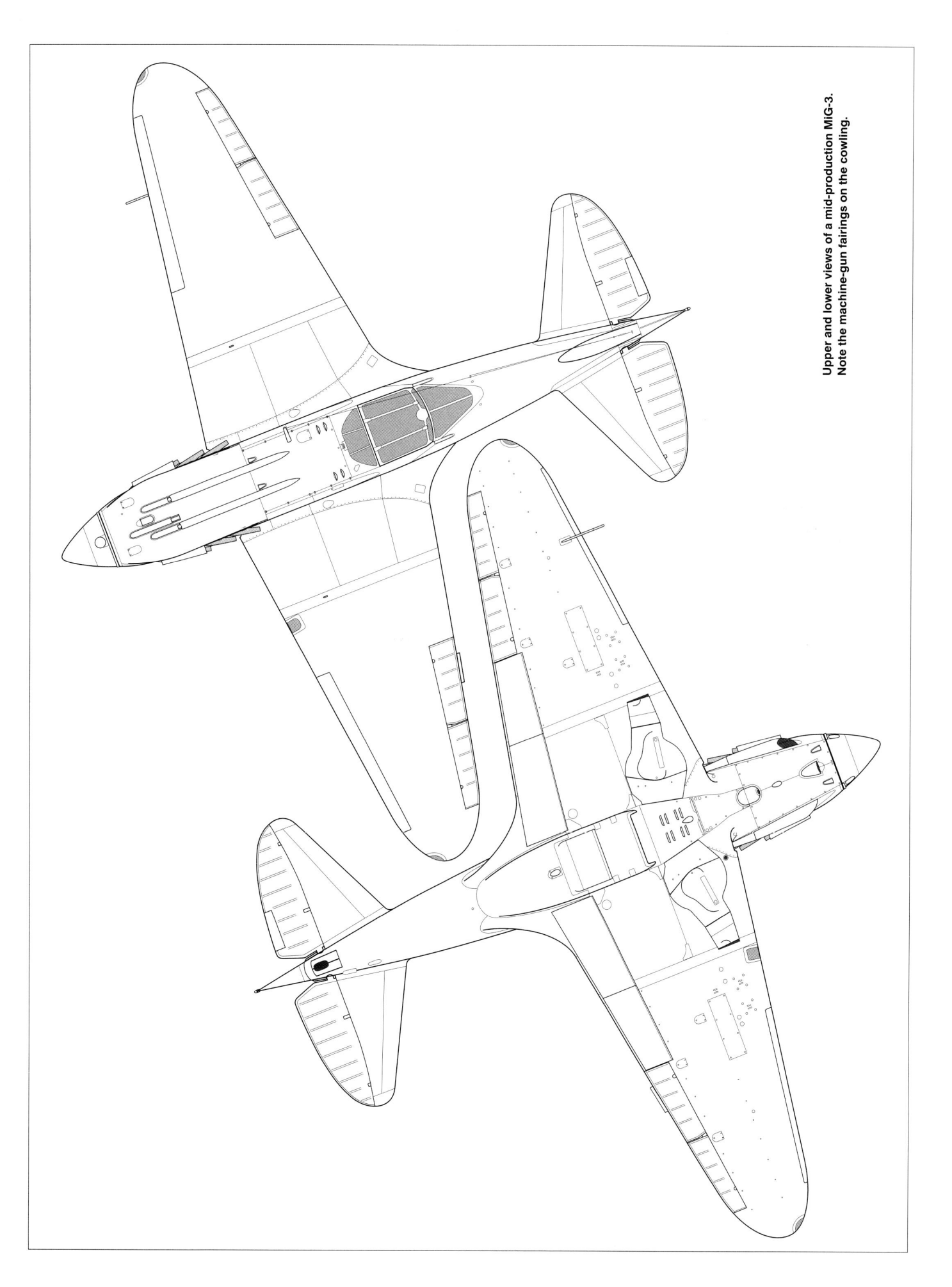

Upper and lower views of a mid-production MiG-3. Note the machine-gun fairings on the cowling.

The second prototype I-200 (c/n 2).

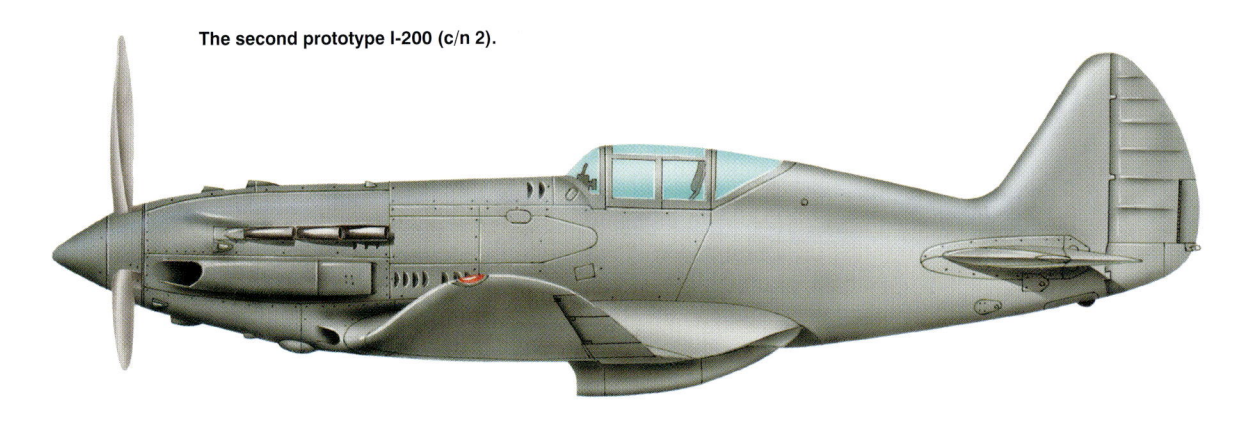

A typical early-production MiG-3 in dark green/dark earth camouflage operated by the 7th IAP (Fighter Regiment) on the Leningrad Front in the summer of 1941.

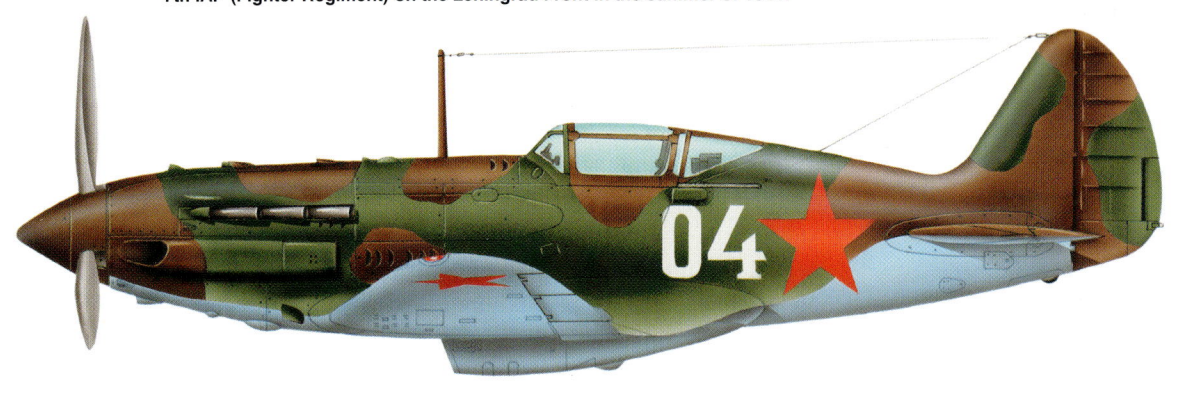

MiG-3 '42 White' (c/n 2267), another 7th IAP aircraft defending Leningrad in October 1941.

A 7th IAP MiG-3 in field-modified camouflage.

Above: A MiG-3 belonging to a Guards unit, as revealed by the *Gvardiya* inscription; apparently the Guards badge was not yet developed at the time.
Below: A MiG-3 operated by the 12th GvIAP (Moscow PVO) in March 1942. Note the red tops of the outer wings.

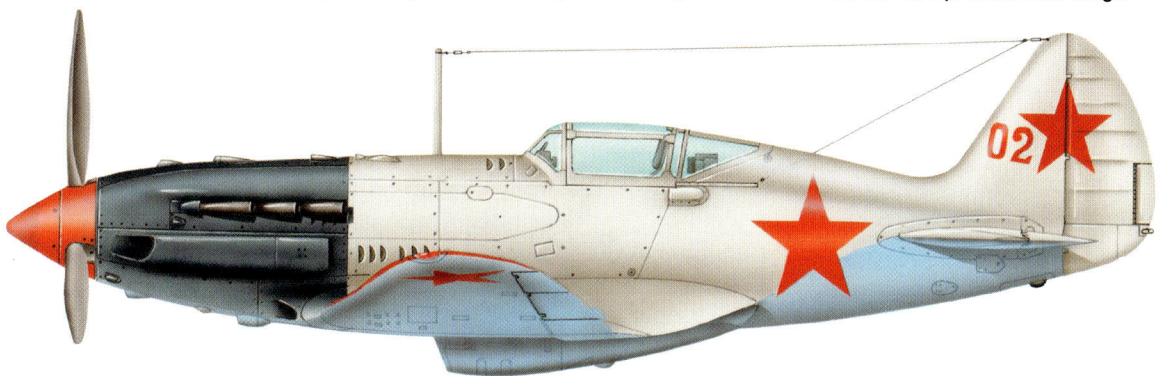

This winter-camouflaged MiG-3 with a red arrow and the legend *Za Rodinu* (For Motherland) was delivered to one of the units in the Moscow Defence District in February 1942. Note the different shape of the colour division line.

Another MiG-3 operated by the same unit and emblazoned *Za Stalina* (For Stalin). Note the RS-82 rockets.

Above: A MiG-3 in late-standard markings with white-outlined stars.
Below: A MiG-3 in typical two-tone green camouflage.

This MiG-3 was captured by Romanian forces in Bessarabia and put into Romanian Air Force service.

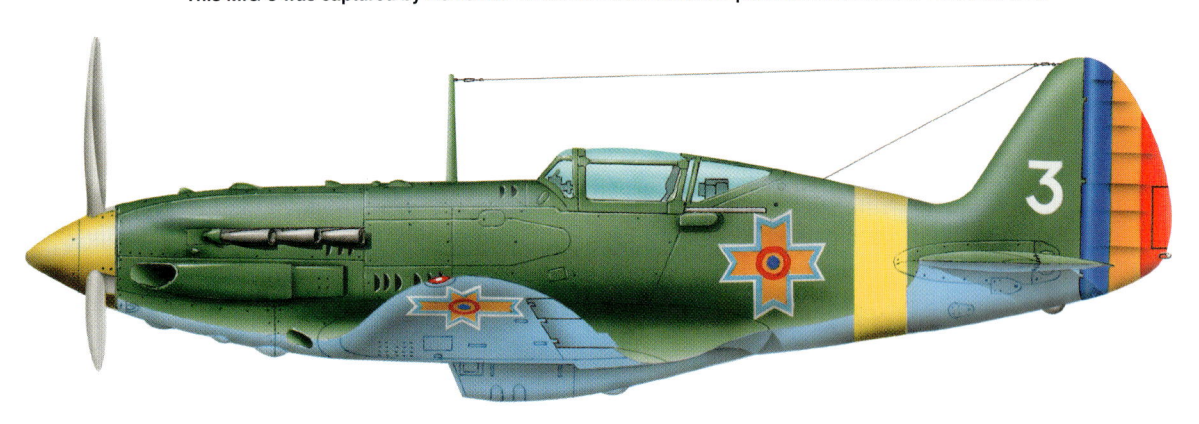

The MiG-9 (MiG-3 M-82) development aircraft.

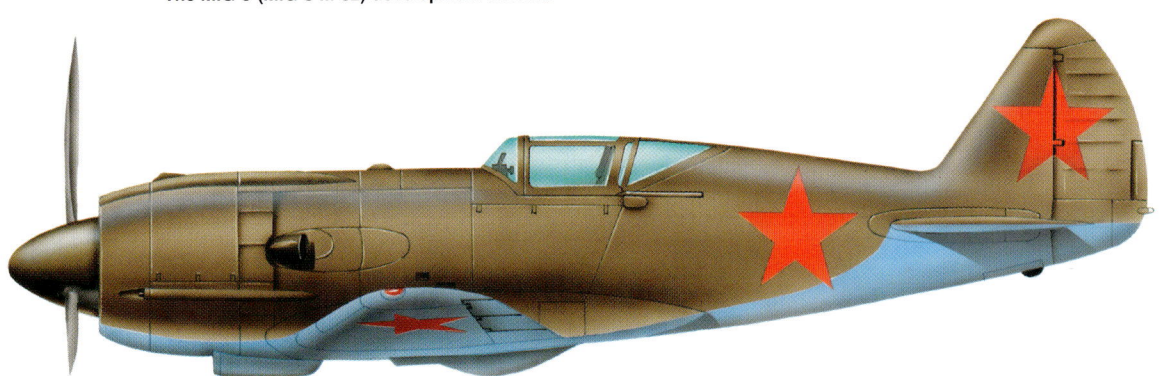

The I-211 development aircraft.

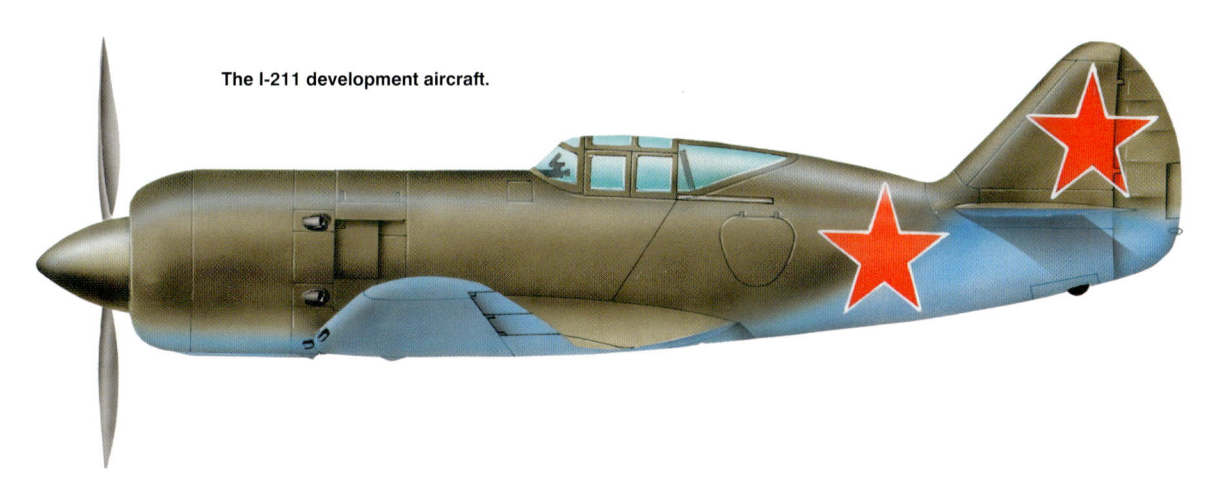

The I-220 high-altitude fighter prototype after refit with an AM-39 engine.

The I-221 high-altitude fighter prototype.

The I-222 high-altitude fighter prototype.

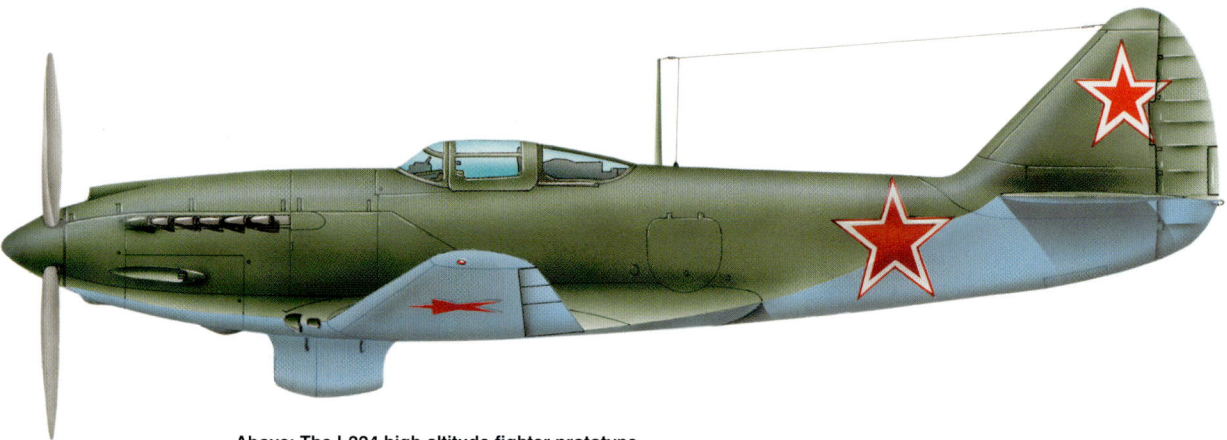

Above: The I-224 high-altitude fighter prototype.
Below: The first prototype of the I-225 high-altitude fighter.

The first prototype of the I-230 (D) fighter.

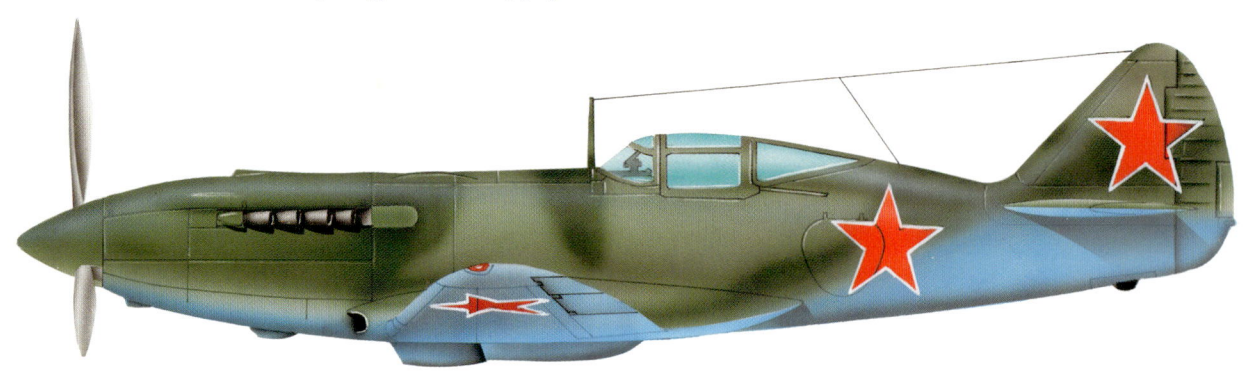

The second prototype of the same aircraft, designated I-231 (2D).

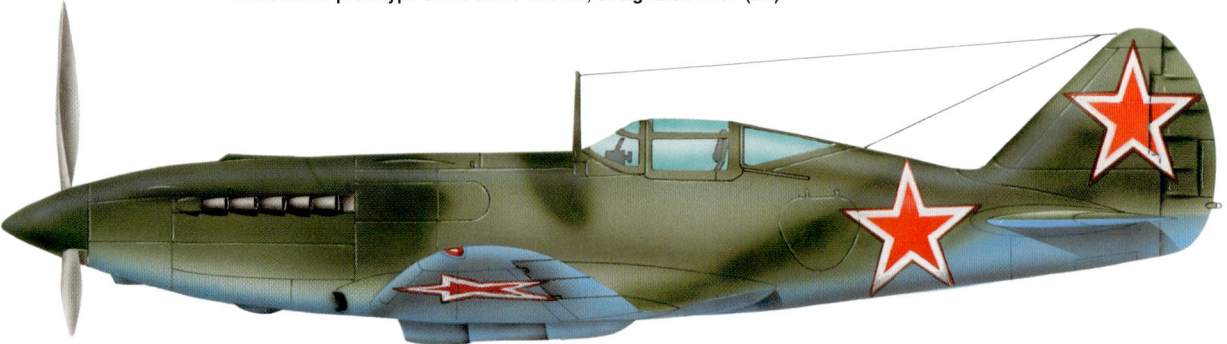

The prototype of the I-250 (N) fighter as originally flown (with a small tail).

The second prototype I-250.

The first prototype of the DIS-200 escort fighter (alias T) with AM-37 in-line engines.

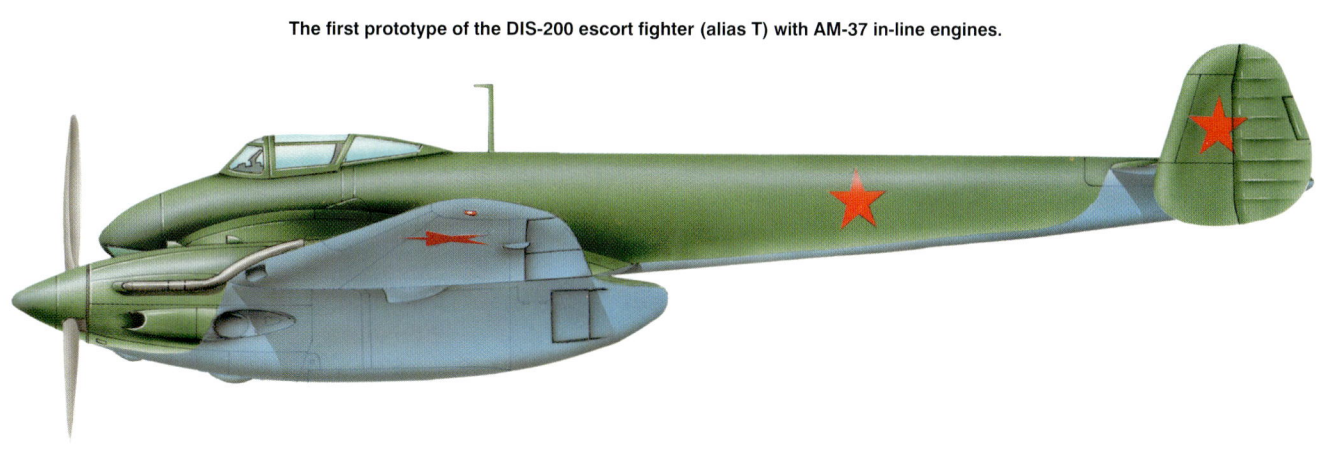

The second DIS-200 (alias IT) with M-82 radials.

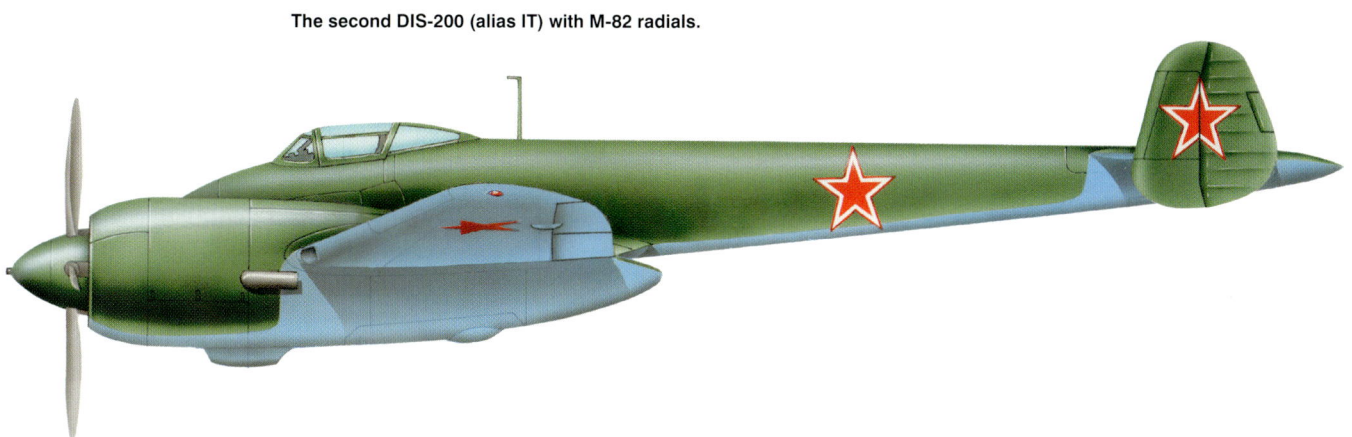

127

We hope you enjoyed this book...

Midland Publishing titles are edited and designed by an experienced and enthusiastic team of specialists.

We always welcome ideas from authors or readers for books they would like to see published.

In addition, our associate, Midland Counties Publications, offers an exceptionally wide range of aviation, military, naval and transport books and videos for sale by mail-order worldwide.

For a copy of the appropriate catalogue, or to order further copies of this book, and any of many other Midland Publishing titles, please write, telephone, fax or e-mail to:

Midland Counties Publications
4 Watling Drive, Hinckley,
Leics, LE10 3EY, England
Tel: (+44) 01455 254 450
Fax: (+44) 01455 233 737
E-mail: midlandbooks@compuserve.com
www.midlandcountiessuperstore.com

US distribution by Specialty Press – see page 2.

Vol.1: Sukhoi S-37 & Mikoyan MFI
1 85780 120 2   £18.95/US $27.95

Vol.2: Flankers: The New Generation
1 85780 121 0   £18.95/US $27.95

Vol.3: Polikarpov's I-16 Fighter
1 85780 131 8   £18.95/US $27.95

Vol.4: Early Soviet Jet Fighters
1 85780 139 3   £19.99/US $29.95

Vol.5: Yakovlev's Piston-Engined Fighters
1 85780 140 7   £19.99/US $29.95

Red Star Volume 6
POLIKARPOV'S BIPLANE FIGHTERS

Yefim Gordon and Keith Dexter

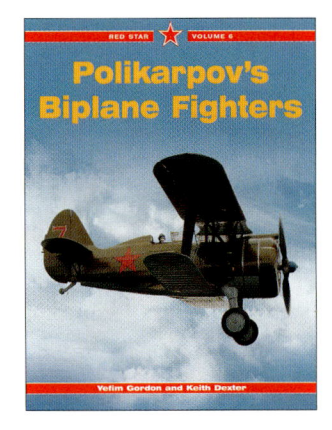

The development of Polikarpov's fighting biplanes including the 2I-N1, the I-3, and I-5, which paved the way for the I-15 which earned fame as the Chato during the Spanish Civil War and saw action against the Japanese; the I-15*bis* and the famous I-153 Chaika retractable gear gull-wing biplane. Details of combat use are given, plus structural descriptions, details of the ill-starred I-190, and of privately owned I-15*bis* and I-153s restored to fly.

Softback, 280 x 215 mm, 128 pages
c250 b/w and colour photos; three-view drawings, 60+ colour side views
1 85780 141 5   **£18.99/US $27.95**

Red Star Volume 7
TUPOLEV Tu-4 SOVIET SUPERFORTRESS

Yefim Gordon and Vladimir Rigmant

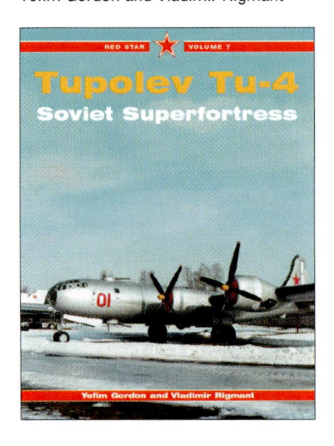

At the end of WW2, three Boeing B-29s fell into Soviet hands; from these came a Soviet copy of this famous bomber in the form of the Tu-4. This examines the evolution of the 'Superfortresski' and its further development into the Tu-70 transport. It also covers the civil airliner version, the Tu-75, and Tu-85, the last of Tupolev's piston-engined bombers. Also described are various experimental versions, including the Burlaki towed fighter programme.

Softback, 280 x 215 mm, 128 pages,
225 black/white and 9 colour photographs, plus line drawings
1 85780 142 3   **£18.99/US $27.95**

Red Star Volume 8
RUSSIA'S EKRANOPLANS
Caspian Sea Monster and other WIG Craft

Sergey Komissarov

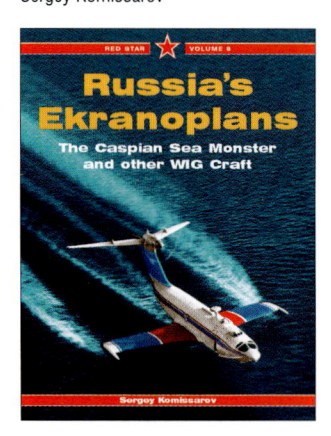

Known as wing-in-ground effect (WIGE) craft or by their Russian name of ekranoplan, these vehicles operate on the borderline between the sky and sea, offering the speed of an aircraft coupled with better operating economics and the ability to operate pretty much anywhere on the world's waterways.

WIGE vehicles by various design bureaus are covered, including the Orlyonok, the only ekranoplan to see squadron service, the Loon and the KM, or Caspian Sea Monster.

Softback, 280 x 215 mm, 128 pages
150 b/w and colour photos, plus dwgs
1 85780 146 6   **£18.99/US $27.95**

Red Star Volume 9
TUPOLEV Tu-160 BLACKJACK
Russia's Answer to the B-1

Yefim Gordon

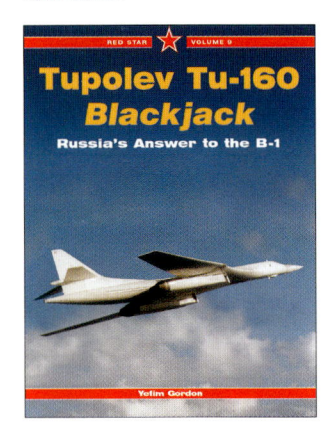

How the Soviet Union's most potent strategic bomber was designed, built and put into service. Comparison is made between the Tu-160 and the Sukhoi T-4 ('aircraft 100', a bomber which was ahead of its time), the variable-geometry 'aircraft 200' – and the Myasishchev M-18 and M-20.

Included are copies of original factory drawings of the Tu-160, M-18, M-20 and several other intriguing projects. Richly illustrated in colour, many shots taken at Engels.

Sbk, 280 x 215 mm, 128pp, 193 col & b/w photos, dwgs, colour side views
1 85780 147 4   **£18.99/US $27.95**

Red Star Volume 10
LAVOCHKIN'S PISTON-ENGINED FIGHTERS

Yefim Gordon

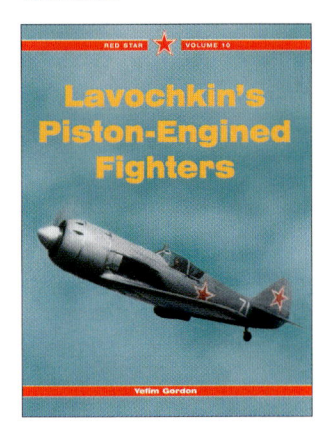

Covers the formation and early years of OKB-301, the design bureau created by Lavochkin, Gorbunov and Goodkov, shortly before the Great Patriotic War.

It describes all of their piston-engined fighters starting with the LaGG-3 and continues with the legendary La-5 and La-7. Concluding chapters deal with the La-9 and La-11, which saw combat in China and Korea in the 1940/50s.

Illustrated with numerous rare and previously unpublished photos drawn from Russian military archives.

Sbk, 280 x 215 mm, 144pp, 274 b/w & 10 col photos, 9pp col views, plus dwgs
1 85780 151 2   **£19.99/US $32.95**

Red Star Volume 11
MYASISHCHEV M-4 and 3M
The First Soviet Strategic Jet Bomber

Yefim Gordon

The story of the Soviet Union's first intercontinental jet bomber, the Soviet answer to the Boeing B-52. The new bomber had many innovative features (including a bicycle landing gear) and was created within an unprecedentedly short period of just one year; observers were stunned when the aircraft was formally unveiled at the 1953 May Day parade. The M-4 and the much-improved 3M remained in service for 40 years.

Softback, 280 x 215 mm, 128 pages,
185 b/w, 14pp of colour photographs, plus line drawings
1 85780 152 0   **£18.99/US $29.95**

Red Star Volume 12
ANTONOV'S TURBOPROP TWINS – An-24/26/30/32

Yefim Gordon

The twin-turboprop An-24 was designed in the late 1950s and was produced by three Soviet aircraft factories; many remain in operation.

The An-24 airliner evolved first into the 'quick fix' An-24T and then into the An-26. This paved the way for the 'hot and high' An-32 and the 'big head' An-30, the latter for aerial photography.

This book lists all known operators of Antonov's twin-turboprop family around the world.

Softback, 280 x 215 mm, 128 pages
c200 colour and black/white photos, plus line drawings
1 85780 153 9   Summer 2003   c**£18.99**